Pearson's CANAL COMPAN…

FOUR COUNTIES RING

S

THE FOUR COUNTIES RING is one of the most picturesque cruising routes available for canal holidays. It wends its way through the rolling farmland West Staffordshire, into Shropshire and the lovely old wn of Market Drayton, down into the dairylands of heshire, past the old salt towns of Nantwich and iddlewich, back up into Staffordshire, through The otteries to the smiling meadowlands of the upper Trent, mpleting the circle by skirting Cannock Chase and tering the new county of West Midlands. Few canal yages encompass such a broad variety of moods and ages. So whether you yearn for open spaces or the rich dustrial archaeology of The Potteries; whether you want to ead the towpath, explore by boat or perhaps just sample e delights of the canalside pubs, we think you will find this w Canal Companion invaluable.

Produced by Michael & Jackie Pearson for J.M. Pearson & Son,
38 Saint Pauls Street West, Burton-on-Trent, Staffordshire DE14 2EW.

ISBN 0 907864 00 7

Typesetting by P.D.R. Typesetting Ltd, 215 Fosse Road North, Leicester LE3 5EZ.
Printed by Taylor-Bloxham Ltd, Nugent Street, Leicester LE3 5HH.

Cover photograph: Tixall Wide, August 1981.

Getting Afloat

Hugh Potter — Editor of the popular monthly "Waterways World" — offers some sound advice for newcomers to canal holidays.

Because canals were built for boats and boats were built for canals, there is simply no better way to explore and appreciate these waterways than from a boat. You can cruise when you like and stop when you like, be it at village, pub, town or in the heart of the countryside, yet you always have your 'home' with you.

There are three types of boat available for holidays on the FOUR COUNTIES RING: self-steer hire boats, hotel boats and camping boats. All may be booked on a weekly basis and the best time to start thinking about a holiday is late in the previous year. From October onwards, companies have their brochures available and will be starting to take bookings. The sooner you book, the greater chance you have of getting the boat you want for the weeks you want.

By far the most popular are the self-steer hire boats which will be seen cruising The Ring from early spring to late autumn and even into the winter. These boats are purpose built along the lines of the traditional working narrowboats, but have all modern conveniences on board: hot and cold running water, shower, flushing toilet, full-size cooker, fridge, heating, and sleeping bags or equivalent bedding. If you've never been on board a modern hire cruiser, you'll be surprised at how much can be fitted in!

When you arrive for your holiday, the hire base staff will explain all the workings of the boat and take you for a trial run until you feel that you have mastered the simple basics of navigation. From then on you'll be 'on your own': starting, stopping and steering the boat, working the locks and catering for yourselves (although there are plenty of canalside eating places as you'll see from this guide).

Opposite you'll see listed the main booking agencies, whilst details of independent hire firms are given under *Boatyards* on the relevant map inside. The hire companies are the people who actually run the boats; some use agencies to take bookings, whilst others prefer to operate independently. A group of 'top notch' independent operators has recently formed 'The Blue Riband Club', membership of which guarantees that their boats have been surveyed to very exacting standards aimed at customer comfort as well as the safety standards to which all hire boats must comply. So how do you choose the right hire boat?

The first thing to do is to write or phone the agencies and the hire companies in the area you want to start your cruise. From the pile of glossy brochures, you'll find that the number of berths available ranges from 2 to 12 and the price of the boat in general increases with the number of berths. Some hirers prefer to spend extra by hiring, say, a 6-berth boat for 4 people, thus providing extra space. A simple comparison of boat lengths will give you a fair idea of the space available. On the other hand, a smaller boat with more berths will probably cost less per person; it all depends on your priorities. All hire rates are lower outside school holidays and, for larger groups, don't forget that one 8-berth will be cheaper than two 4-berths.

Prices vary for similar boats from different companies, so look carefully at the small print to see that is included and what will be extra. VAT is usually extra; gas for cooking and heating is free; but fuel, car parking, pets, TV and cancellation insurance depend on the company.

Remember that glossy brochures and high prices do not always mean super luxury boats and, equally, that low prices and black and white brochures do not necessarily mean poor quality.
Short list the boats with the right number of double and single berths in the right cabins. Remember that young children will probably need to go to bed before adults; a separate cabin at one end of the boat is ideal.

When you have your list, the best way of deciding which boat to choose is to phone up the boatyards and go and see the boats. Only in this way can you really appreciate the differences between different companies' boats. Whilst you're there, ask to hear the engine running. Some are excellently quiet, some can be rather noisy; the quieter the better for the enjoyment of your holiday.
If you're not able to visit the boatyards, then it would be worth checking through back issues of the monthly magazine *Waterways World* which regularly features detailed hire boat reviews.
For those who prefer to be 'looked after' — meals cooked, locks worked etc — there are the hotel boats. As the name suggests, these offer hotel-style accommodation on board a pair of narrowboats. They run to a fixed itinerary and thus can be joined for a particular route. They are especially suited to single people, as there will be ample company on board. Contact the Boat Enquiries agency for details of hotel boats.
Finally, camping boats offer 'rough and ready' accommodation, at low cost,

usually in traditional narrowboats. They are ideal for school parties, scouts, guides etc and usually cater for 12 per boat. They offer a boatman to take charge of the boat, framed bunks under a canvas awning, plus basic cooking and washing facilities. Willow Wren (see Map 14) operate camping boats on the FOUR COUNTIES RING.
Then, of course, you might think of buying a boat, but don't consider this until you've had some cruising experience on hire boats or with friends. A wide variety of boats, new and secondhand, grp (glass-fibre) and steel, are always available and *Waterways World, Canal & Riverboat* and *Exchange & Mart* always have a good selection for sale. Several finance companies specialise in boats and, typically, offer up to 80% of the purchase price over a maximum of 7 years. If you're buying a boat through a boatyard, they'll be able to recommend a finance company, but if not go back to those magazine ads.
Before buying, check that the dimensions of the boat are right (page 48), make sure that you can find a mooring and, when considering finances, take into account maintenance and running costs, insurance, mooring fees and cruising licences.
But whichever way you choose to get afloat, there's no doubting that you'll enjoy your holiday on the FOUR COUNTIES RING. Happy cruising!

Boat Booking Agencies
Blakes. Tel: Wroxham (06053) 3226 (brochure); 2915 (bookings).
Boat Enquiries. Tel: Oxford (0865) 511161.
Hoseasons. Tel: Lowestoft (0502) 62101 (brochure); 67511 (bookings).

Cowley Cutting

1 SHROPSHIRE UNION CANAL Barbridge Junction 40mls/18hrs

AUTHERLEY IS ONE OF THE FOUR JUNCTIONS where those 'doing' 'The Ring' have to turn off the canal they have been cruising onto fresh waters. Here, clockwise travellers of the FOUR COUNTIES RING leave the Staffs & Worcs Canal, turning right under the roving bridge and into the shallow stop lock on their way to the Shropshire Union Canal. Anti-clockwise travellers leave 'The Shroppie' and turn left into the Staffs & Worcs Canal which they follow as far as Great Haywood (see Map 28).

Despite the threatening proximity of Wolverhampton, Autherley, like many canal junctions, is a self-contained, out of the way place. The old boatmen called it 'Cut End' because the Shropshire Union ended here. There were toll offices, stables and canal employees cottages here, and a constant procession of narrowboats locking through the stop lock dividing the two companies precious water supplies. Nowadays it's still a thriving canal junction, with two boatyards disgorging hire boats at weekends, and plenty of pleasure boats passing through on their way to all points of the canal compass.

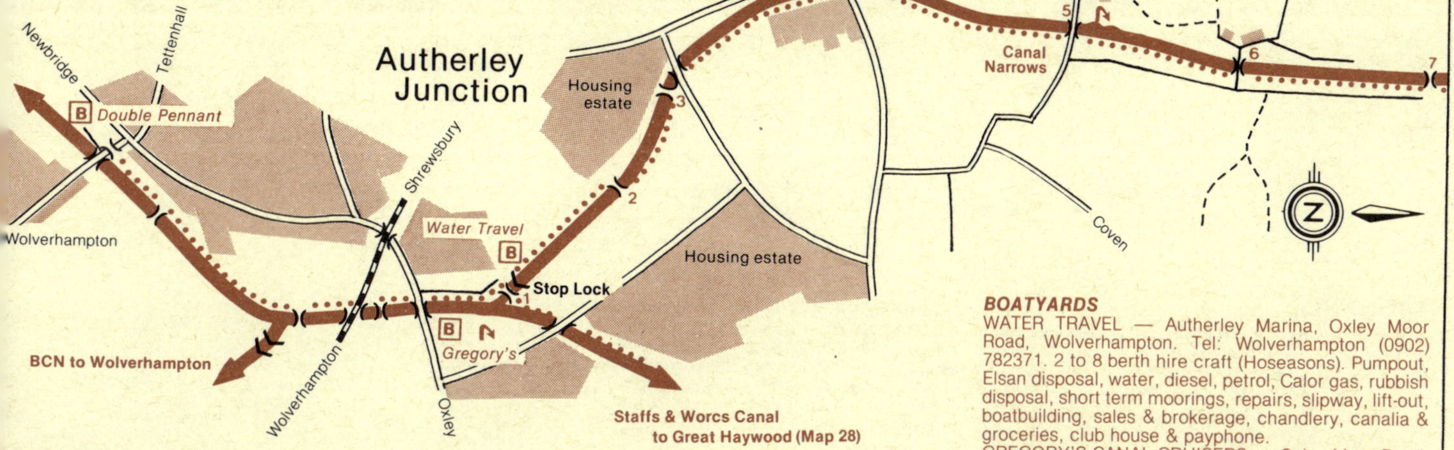

AUTHERLEY JUNCTION

EATING & DRINKING

No nearby pubs, but boaters are welcome at Water Travel's licensed club house.

SHOPPING

No shops as such but a good range of frozen foods and groceries available at Water Travel's shop.

PUBLIC TRANSPORT

BUSES — From Oxley Moor road bridge (beside Gregory's boatyard) frequent WMPTE service to/from Wolverhampton. Tel: Wolverhampton (0902) 20018.

BOATYARDS

WATER TRAVEL — Autherley Marina, Oxley Moor Road, Wolverhampton. Tel: Wolverhampton (0902) 782371. 2 to 8 berth hire craft (Hoseasons). Pumpout, Elsan disposal, water, diesel, petrol, Calor gas, rubbish disposal, short term moorings, repairs, slipway, lift-out, boatbuilding, sales & brokerage, chandlery, canalia & groceries, club house & payphone.

GREGORY'S CANAL CRUISERS — Oxley Moor Road, Autherley Junction, Wolverhampton. Tel: Wolverhampton (0902) 783070. 4-12 berth hire craft (Blakes). Pumpout, Calor gas, repairs.

DOUBLE PENNANT — Hordern Road, Wolverhampton. Tel: Wolverhampton (0902) 753453. 2 to 8 berth hire craft (Hoseasons). Water, diesel, Calor gas, rubbish disposal, moorings, repairs & servicing, slipway, boat sales & brokerage, chandlery & canalia.

2 SHROPSHIRE UNION CANAL 3mls/1hr Autherley Jnct — Barbridge Jnct 36mls/17hrs

THE SHROPSHIRE UNION CANAL slices through the Staffordshire countryside by way of a series of cuttings and embankments typical of the bold, 19th century designs of Thomas Telford, who engineered the route between Autherley and Nantwich, originally known as the Birmingham & Liverpool Junction Canal. Earlier canal builders preferred to follow the contours of the landscape, and this resulted in much more winding routes.

There are two notable structures on this section either side of the pretty village of Brewood. To the South the distinctly ornate balustraded Avenue Bridge (No.10) was built thus to take the carriageway to Chillington Hall. The advent of the canals heralded many such attempts at ornamentation and disguise, where powerful landowners would only grant permission for the new waterway to pierce their demesne if suitable steps were taken to adorn the purely functional architecture of the new trade route. In contrast, to the North of Brewood, Telford's canal had to cross over his London-Holyhead road, rebuilt by the great engineer in 1830 along an old Turnpike that had once been the Roman's Watling Street. The crossing is made on a sturdy, yet elegant, iron & stone aqueduct inscribed 1832.

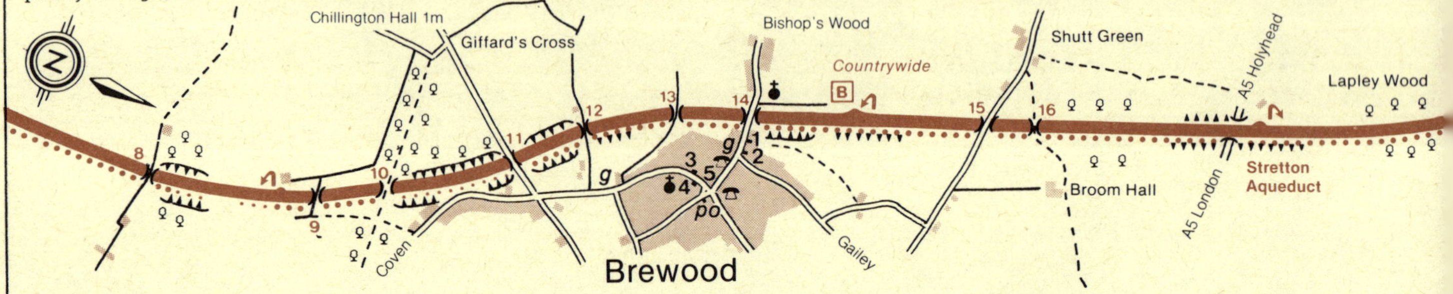

BREWOOD

A lovely village, almost a small town, retaining an ancient air of calm. Doubtless because it has the luck to be a mile South of the A5, and we suspect few of the set-jawed hurriers along that artery ever stray to hilltop 'Brood' as the locals call it. Winding lanes lead to a centre with some fine buildings, notably the Gothick fantasies of Speedwell Castle at the edge of the Market Place, built in the 18th century from the winnings on a racehorse called Speedwell. The parish church of St Mary & St Chad dates from the 13th century, but has contributions from many others. Inside are alabaster monuments to the local Giffords.

EATING & DRINKING

BRIDGE INN (1) — Ansells & bar snacks

LAVELLE'S RESTAURANT (3) — Dinner Mon, Tue, Thur-Sat, Sat & Sun lunch; bookings Brewood 850529; Sunday lunch from £4.95, dinner from £6.25.

Other pubs to choose from in centre (5).

SHOPPING

EC Wed (partial).

All kinds of shops, plus Lloyds Bank (2), within 5 mins of Bridge 14.

The 'Studio One' (4) craft shop has a good selection of sensible and worthwhile crafts, many of local origin. Light snacks are available.

PLACES TO VISIT

CHILLINGTON HALL — 1½m W of Br 10. Open Thur May-mid Sep, Sun Aug; 2.30-5.30; admission 60p adults, 30p children. Georgian house with grounds by Capability Brown. Tel: Brewood 850236.

PUBLIC TRANSPORT

BUSES — From Market Place: (5) Warstone's/Midland Red 877/8, hourly Mon-Sat, to/from Wolverhampton. Warstone's 471, 2-3 per day, to/from Penkridge & Cannock. Tel: Cheslyn Hay (0922) 414141.

Warstone's Green Buses are almost in the vintage category — a real treat for bus buffs!

BOATYARDS

COUNTRYWIDE CRUISERS — The Wharf, Brewood, Staffs ST19 9BG. Tel: Brewood (0902) 850166. 4 to 8 berth hire craft (Blue Riband Club). Pumpout, diesel, water, calor gas, repairs, engine sales, slipway, moorings, groceries & canalia.

3 SHROPSHIRE UNION CANAL — 6mls/2½hrs Autherley Jnct — Barbridge Jnct 32mls/15hrs

PASSING THROUGH THE SOLITARY LOCK at Wheaton Aston — Northbound it's 17 miles to the next one! — the relentless straights of the old Birmingham & Liverpool Junction are punctuated only twice by gentle curves, and the canal runs typically above the adjoining farmland upon an embankment or deep in a mysterious wooded cutting.

How astonishingly remote and unpeopled the landscape is! The West Midland conurbation lies less than 10 miles to the South, yet moor for the night in open country between Weaton Aston and Little Onn, and you'll have only the occasional hoot of an owl and the distant wash of headlights upon a country lane for company.

The abandoned aerodrome near Little Onn was a wartime bomber base. Locals recall the droning squadrons of Lancasters and Wellingtons taking off at dusk on their way to bomb Germany. It all seems rather unreal today. No more agonised watching of the radar at dawn to count them home, no more NAFFI dances in Nissen huts, only the learner driver out on the mossy runway.

Another well remembered wartime incident on this part of the canal occurred at Wheaton Aston Lock. A Fellows Morton narrowboat travelling southwards on a moonlit night carrying an unsheeted cargo of shining aluminium, was spotted by a German bomber — presumably straying from the bigger targets of Wolverhampton and Birmingham — which unleashed a bomb that exploded less than a hundred yards from the lock!

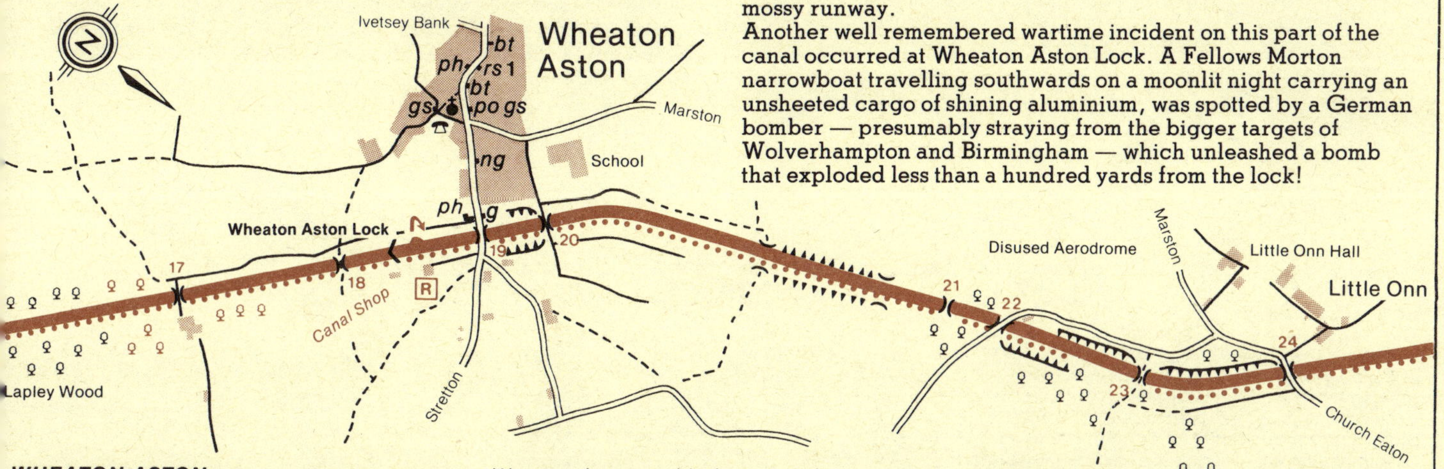

WHEATON ASTON

Hopelessly residential. The breathing space between the older cottages and farm buildings being relentlessly plugged by new housing. Yet not all the former charm has been forfeited and there are reminders of a prettier past — a donkey tethered by an old barn, an elegant Victorian church, an old fashioned village garage, and the occasional passage of one of Warstone's venerable buses on its way down the dusty lanes to such buccolic destinations as Ivetsey Bank or The Rookery.

EATING & DRINKING

HARTLEY ARMS — canalside by Bridge 19, Bank's, lunches Mon-Sat & bar snacks.

TREVETT HOUSE (1) — breakfast, morning coffee & lunch (daily ex Mon), plus evening carvery on Thur-Sat. Book for latter: Wheaton Aston (0785) 840707.

SHOPPING

Post Office, general stores, baker, butchers, news-agent & grocery 5 minutes from canal at Bridge 19. Most shops seem to close for lunch 1-2pm.

PUBLIC TRANSPORT

BUSES — From village centre: Warstone's/Midland Red 877/878, 3 per day Mon-Sat, to/from Wolver-hampton. Warstone's 471, 2-3 per day Mon-Sat, to/from Brewood, Penkridge & Cannock. Tel: Cheslyn Hay (0922) 414141.

DEEP, SHADOWY SANDSTONE CUTTINGS, spanned by lichened grey stone bridges of great balance and beauty, lead to the eighty-one unlined yards of Cowley Tunnel — the Shropshire Union's only tunnel. Telford and his contractor William Provis had intended the tunnel to be much longer — 690 yards in fact. But the sandstone proved so treacherously brittle that all but the remaining short section was opened out.

On a clear day the embankment between Bridges 36 & 37 offers views of that famous Shropshire landmark, The Wrekin, 15 miles to the South-west; a slumbering whaleback of a summit, 1,335 feet high. A. E. Housman immortalised it in 'A Shropshire Lad', and Salopians raise their glasses 'To all friends around the Wrekin'. They say you can see seventeen counties from the top. The dismantled railway line which crossed the canal at Gnosall connected Stafford with Wellington. It was unusual in that it was actually built by the Shropshire Union Canal Company, in an apparent attempt to hedge their bets on whichever mode of transport, waterway or railway, would outlast the other. When in 1846 they leased themselves to the London & North Western Railway, there can have been few shareholders who would have backed the canal to outlast the railway as it has done!

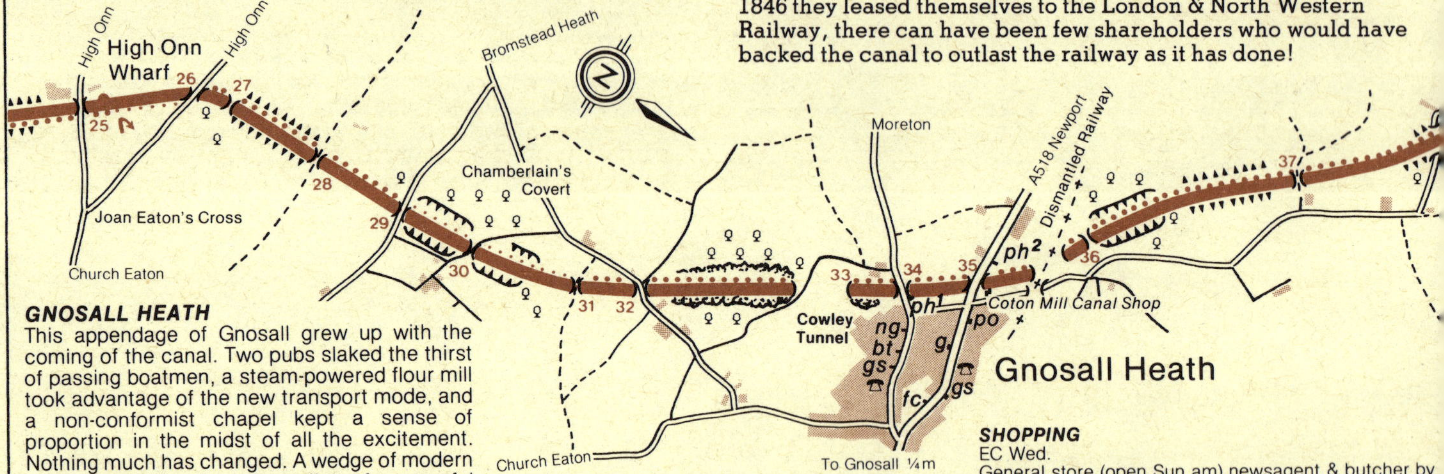

GNOSALL HEATH

This appendage of Gnosall grew up with the coming of the canal. Two pubs slaked the thirst of passing boatmen, a steam-powered flour mill took advantage of the new transport mode, and a non-conformist chapel kept a sense of proportion in the midst of all the excitement. Nothing much has changed. A wedge of modern housing provides the *raison d'etre* for a useful row of shops by Bridge 34, the pubs now pander to pleasure boaters and motorists, the flour mill is a canal souvenir and craft shop and the chapel is a hardware store.

Gnosall itself lies half a mile to the East. The church is substantial, largely 13th century, though we found it locked. Oh, and by the way, you don't pronounce the 'G'!

EATING & DRINKING

THE BOAT (1) — Marstons. Lunchtime pizzas (not Wed); burgers in the evenings. Bar billiards & canalside garden.

THE NAVIGATION (2) — Courage & lunchtime bar food.

Fish & chips — open Mon-Sat lunch & evening except Mon lunch.

SHOPPING

EC Wed.

General store (open Sun am) newsagent & butcher by Bridge 34. PO by Bridge 35. More shops (including Barclays Bank open 10-2.30 Mon-Fri) in Gnosall.

PUBLIC TRANSPORT

BUSES — From A518, Bridge 35: Happy Days coaches, hourly Mon-Sat to/from Stafford & Newport. Tel: Woodseaves (078 574) 231.

Newport is a pleasant old town with remains of former Norbury-Shrewsbury Canal; journey time by bus 10 mins.

There Went The Boats

15 YEARS have passed since narrowboats carried freight regularly on the Shropshire Union Canal. These evocative photographs, taken by Mike Webb in the Sixties, capture something of the old atmosphere of a working canal in the last sad years of commercial carrying.

1/2: Audlem Locks in 1967. The motorboat *Tarporley* and its butty *Beverley* descend the flight with cargoes of copper sludge from Darleston, Wolverhampton, to Manchester Docks for export to Canada. Taking a 'pair' through single narrow locks was always a complicated affair involving expert use of the tow line. In this instance, however, we can clearly see that the butty is being bow-hauled between the closely spaced locks by the Captain as his wife steers.

3: Another load of copper sludge for Canada — what did they do with it all? This time the boat is *Trout,* the location Brewood and the year 1965.

4: Tyrley Locks, 1967. A pair of boats belonging to the ill-fated Birmingham & Midland Co who tried in vain to establish new traffics during the final years. The motor boat in the lock is *Yeoford,* the butty waiting its turn *Ash*. They're bound for Liverpool with aluminium loaded in Walsall.

1

2

3

4

Keeping the Cut Open!

Next time you pass through Norbury Junction spare a thought for the British Waterways Board Section Inspector Mr Dean and his thirty staff who have 40 miles of canal, 6 reservoirs and numerous feeder channels to maintain!

For the purposes of administration and maintenance British Waterways Board canals are divided into 'sections' — if you're cruising 'The Ring' you'll pass through 4 different ones. Norbury Junction is headquarters of the Norbury Section which includes the Shropshire Union and Staffs & Worcs canals between Audlem and Gailey, plus the reservoirs at Belvide, Calf Heath and Gailey which keep this section of canal topped up with water.
Dredging is one of the most important activities required to keep the canal open to traffic, and at Norbury there's a gang of 4 men permanently engaged in operating the dredging fleet. There's a good chance you'll come across them on your cruise and see the mechanical dredger *Stoat* scooping up silt from the bed of the canal and loading it into the hoppers which are taken by the tugs to a suitable dumping point — often an old marl pit or nearby field, if the local farmer's friendly!
Steel piling is being put in on many sections of canal to combat bank erosion caused by the passage of motor boats, and Norbury has two teams currently working their way along the 80 miles of banking between Audlem and Gailey. Lock maintenance is a crucial activity on any waterway, and at Norbury there are carpenters and bricklayers whose job it is to keep the locks in good working order. In the winter when the canal is closed for maintenance, the carpenters come out of their cosy workshop and help to fit new gates and paddles, whilst the bricklayers will be busy repointing the masonry of the lock chambers.
Most of the locks in the Norbury Section are grouped in the flights at Tryley, Adderley and Audlem, and at each of these places there's a resident lock-keeper. But they aren't there to operate the locks for passing boaters — those days are gone! Nowadays the lock-keepers have to keep the lock gear in good condition, to check water levels, keep the banks and towpaths clear, mow the grass, and cut the hedges.
Most of the men employed by the Norbury Section live locally, many in the BWB cottages at the Junction itself. There are still a good number of well known canal family names in the team. Names like Till and Blunn which seem to have worked on the canal since it was built! Mr Dean himself has been on the canals for 43 years, beginning as an apprentice carpenter at Norbury when the canal belonged to the LMS railway!

A recent occurence at Norbury is typical of the kind of emergencies which can crop up suddenly on the canals. A farmer whose fields adjoin the canal near Gnosall discovered water seeping into his pasture beside the canal embankment. It was late in the evening, but he managed to get through to one of the Norbury staff, and immediately a band of men from the Norbury cottages went out to the scene of the leakage. They quickly put in stop planks at the bridges either side of the embankment, isolating a mile of canal. In the meantime Mr Dean was alerted and he telephoned the area office at Northwich who in turn called the BWB headquarters in London, the latter, so that they could put out a warning on Canalphone and inform all the hire-boat firms whose boats were likely to use that section of canal. Two Norbury men stayed all night at the embankment, and in the morning they had to report that the situation was deteriorating, and that more water was pouring out into the adjoining fields. And so the canal was quickly closed off as far as Norbury and the suspect section drained of water. It eventually took a week of hard work and 300 tons of clay to plug the leak. Doubtless holidaymakers who'd planned to cruise 'The Shroppie' that week were disappointed. But the quick action of the Norbury men saved a much more serious breach from occuring, and their vigilance kept the cut open for the rest of the holiday cruising season!

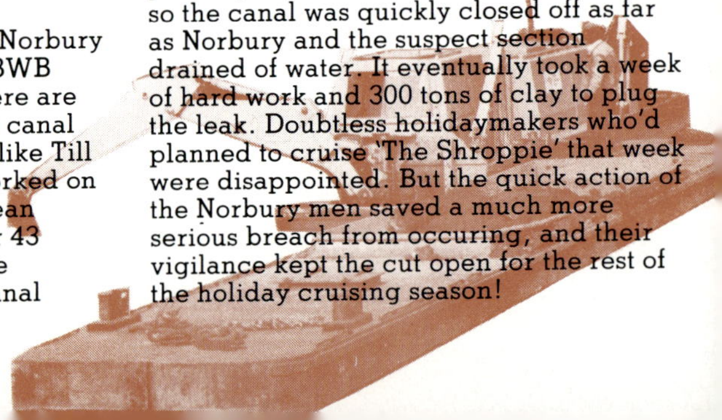

5 SHROPSHIRE UNION CANAL

15mls/5½hrs Autherley Jnct — Barbridge Jnct 23mls/11hrs

THERE ARE TWO MAGNIFICENT engineering achievements and a famous former canal junction on this section. Shelmore embankment (the canal builders called it The Great Bank) proved the most troublesome part of the canal to construct due to constant slipping of the earthworks, and yet it need not have been built at all if Lord Anson of Norbury Park had allowed a more direct course across his land. It was eventually completed in 1835 after six years of toil. The adjoining country road tunnels under it twice.

On the other side of Norbury Junction lies Grub Street cutting. For over a mile the canal is enveloped in a sinister belt of vegetation of almost jungle proportions which had us thinking of the waterway that penetrates Conrad's 'Heart of Darkness'. At the southern end of the cutting the A519 crosses the canal on an unusual double-arched bridge which supports what must be the tiniest telegraph pole in England. A black, monkey-like creature is reputed to have haunted this bridge since a boatman was drowned here in the 1800s.

Norbury Junction is the spot from where a branch canal ran to the earlier East-Shropshire system of 'tub-boat' canals which linked the collieries, ironworks and quarries of Ironbridge and Coalbrookdale. A branch of a branch led to Shrewsbury, crossing the river Tern at Longdon upon the first cast-iron aqueduct ever built — designed by the ubiquitous Thomas Telford.

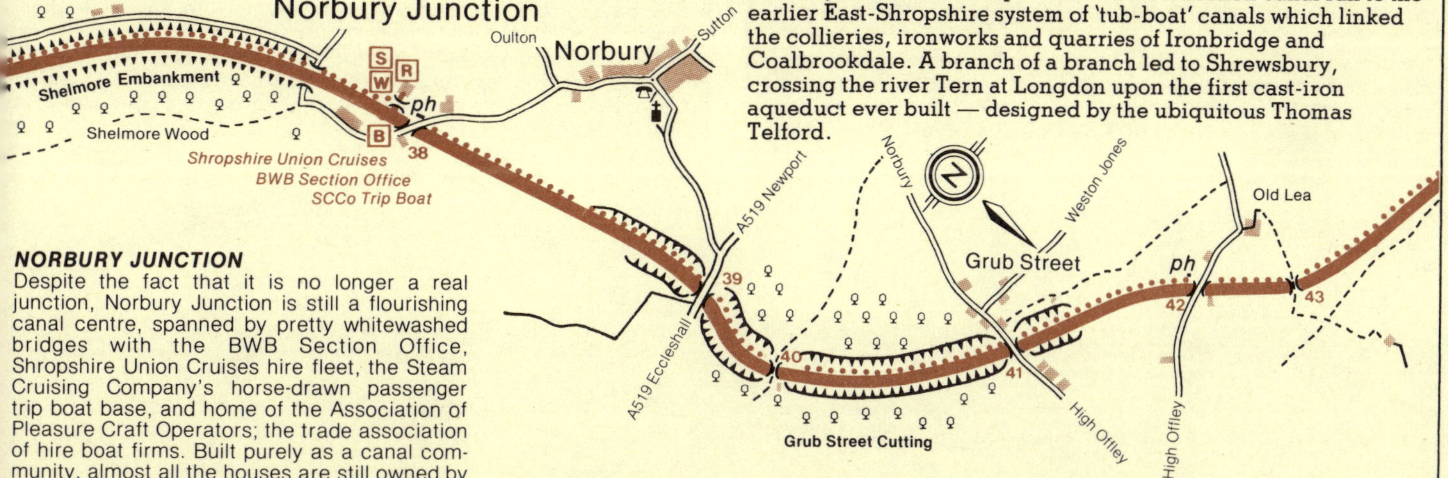

NORBURY JUNCTION

Despite the fact that it is no longer a real junction, Norbury Junction is still a flourishing canal centre, spanned by pretty whitewashed bridges with the BWB Section Office, Shropshire Union Cruises hire fleet, the Steam Cruising Company's horse-drawn passenger trip boat base, and home of the Association of Pleasure Craft Operators; the trade association of hire boat firms. Built purely as a canal community, almost all the houses are still owned by the British Waterways Board, and many of the men who work on the canal still live here.

EATING & DRINKING

The Junction Inn — Free house, bar lunches & evening grills Mon-Sat. Canalside Bridge 38.

SHOPPING

Groceries at Shropshire Union Cruises, open daily.

BOATYARDS

SHOPSHIRE UNION CRUISES — The Wharf, Norbury Junction, Stafford ST20 0PN. Tel: Woodseaves (078574) 292. 2-12 berth hire craft (Blakes). Pumpout, diesel, petrol, moorings, repairs & servicing, drydock, slipway, chandlery, canalia & groceries.

HIGH OFFLEY

EATING & DRINKING

THE ANCHOR — Free house, sandwiches to order. Canalside Bridge 42. *An old boatman's pub surviving almost unchanged from narrowboat days. Closed some nights in winter. Tel: Woodseaves 569.*

6 SHROPSHIRE UNION CANAL 19mls/7½hrs Autherley Jnct — Barbridge Jnct 20mls/9½hrs

CROSSING THE BORDER between Staffordshire and Shropshire, the canal continues to traverse unruffled countryside of prosperous farms; an extraordinarily remote region without main roads and where there's never been a railway. Boaters with bicycles aboard can take themselves off exploring the little lanes that lead to Sanbrook, Pickstock, Weston Jones, Outlands, Bishop's Offley and their like.

A mile North of the canal in Knighton Wood there used to be a reservoir built to supply the canal with water but long since abandoned. At Knighton itself, where the Adbaston road crosses the canal, there is a Cadbury factory manufacturing powdered milk. This used to be a busy spot on the canal, for at one time Cadbury's had their own fleet of narrowboats which collected milk churns from farms the length of the Shropshire Union, bringing the milk to Knighton for evaporation, and also carrying the raw materials for cocoa making from Bournville. One can't help feeling rather sad that the chocolate maroon coloured Cadbury boats no longer gather at the incongruously well maintained wharf.

Shebdon embankment carries the canal 50 feet above the surrounding farmland, and you pass by the chimney tops of the little Wharf Inn tucked in at the foot of the embankment opposite a small basin typical of the once numerous agricultural wharves along this canal.

Walkers and boaters may well be treated to one of the inland waterways' most romantic encounters on this section — the idyllic passage of a horse-drawn narrowboat — for the passenger carrying horse-boat *Iona* transports her voluble cargoes regularly between Norbury Junction and Market Drayton. The horse's harness jingles and jangles, his hooves clip and clop, and the boat's bows comb a peaceful parting across the torpid head of canal water.

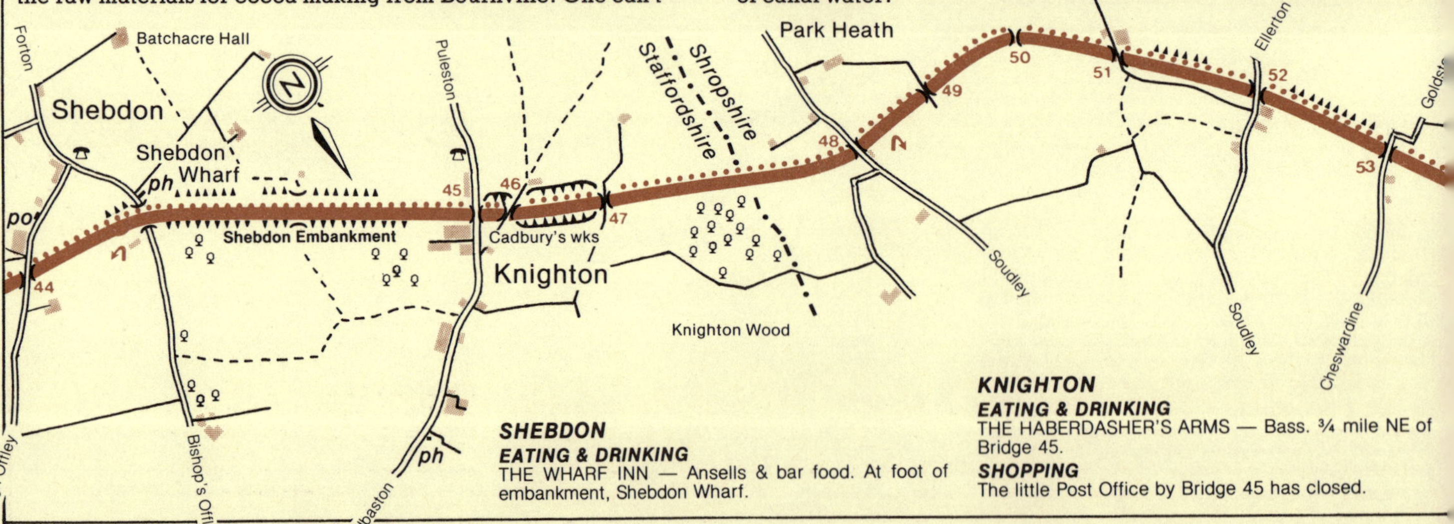

SHEBDON

EATING & DRINKING

THE WHARF INN — Ansells & bar food. At foot of embankment, Shebdon Wharf.

KNIGHTON

EATING & DRINKING

THE HABERDASHER'S ARMS — Bass. ¾ mile NE of Bridge 45.

SHOPPING

The little Post Office by Bridge 45 has closed.

7 SHROPSHIRE UNION CANAL 23mls/8½hrs Autherley Jnct — Barbridge Jnct 16mls/8hrs

BETWEEN BRIDGES 58 & 62 the towpath side of the canal forms the county border, so that for about two miles you are a few feet back inside Staffordshire.

Woodseaves is another prodigious 'Shroppie' cutting, at points almost a hundred feet deep. The cuttings proved almost as troublesome to Telford as the embankments. There were regular avalanches and, even today, though strengthened by the roots of venerable trees, the cutting requires regular maintenance, and is often closed for lengthy periods in winter. A pair of giant bridges cross the cutting as if on stilts. Number 58 has recently been rebuilt and strengthened to good effect.

At Tyrley a flight of five locks — the last southbound for 17 miles! — carry the canal down into or up out of Market Drayton through a dappled sandstone cutting of much beauty. This rocky cutting, rarely touched by sunlight, provides the perfect damp environment for mosses and ferns to flourish in. After dusk bats leave their tree hole roosts to hunt for their diet of insects, acrobatically twisting and turning over the luminous water.

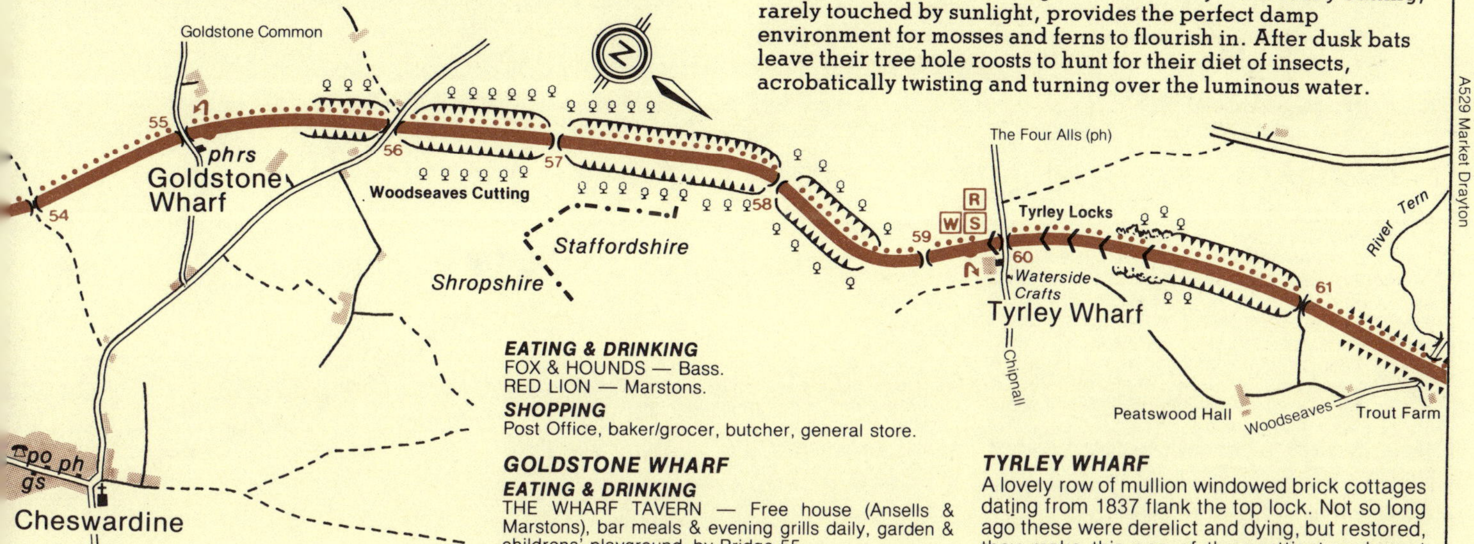

EATING & DRINKING
FOX & HOUNDS — Bass.
RED LION — Marstons.

SHOPPING
Post Office, baker/grocer, butcher, general store.

CHESWARDINE
A small village crowned by a lovely red sandstone church best seen from the foot of the hilly main street.

GOLDSTONE WHARF
EATING & DRINKING
THE WHARF TAVERN — Free house (Ansells & Marstons), bar meals & evening grills daily, garden & childrens' playground, by Bridge 55.
Anyone who has read and loved L.T.C. Rolt's "Narrow Boat" will find the 'simple, friendly' inn, where the horse-boat Captain was sole customer ensconced by an open fire, transformed into a plush and hugely popular hostelry renowned for its food; anathema to those who like THE ANCHOR at High Offley and, of course, vice-versa.

TYRLEY WHARF
A lovely row of mullion windowed brick cottages dating from 1837 flank the top lock. Not so long ago these were derelict and dying, but restored, they make this one of the prettiest and most photographed and painted spots on the canal system. Two exiled Lancastrians, Ken & Lillias Greenhalgh, have opened a marvellous canal craft shop in the end cottage. On no account should this be passed, nearly everything is made locally; no gimmick souvenirs here!

IF THERE ARE PRETTIER and better cared for locks than those at Adderley then we'd like to see them! Lock-keeper Frank Butter regularly wins prizes for the flight, and the locals proudly call it 'Adderley Park'. Flower beds line the banks in profusion and the gravelled towpath crunches beneath the feet of the hurrying lock-wheeler.

Legend has it that Betton Wood is haunted by a shrieking ghost. Certainly the working boat people would never moor here in the old days. Wildlife abounds; shades of the Wild Wood in 'Wind in the Willows'.

N.B. Southbound between Market Drayton and Norbury Junction boaters may meet the horse-drawn passenger boat *Iona*, and if so should pass right to right to avoid the towline. Northbound boaters should encounter no difficulty passing in the normal way; left to left.

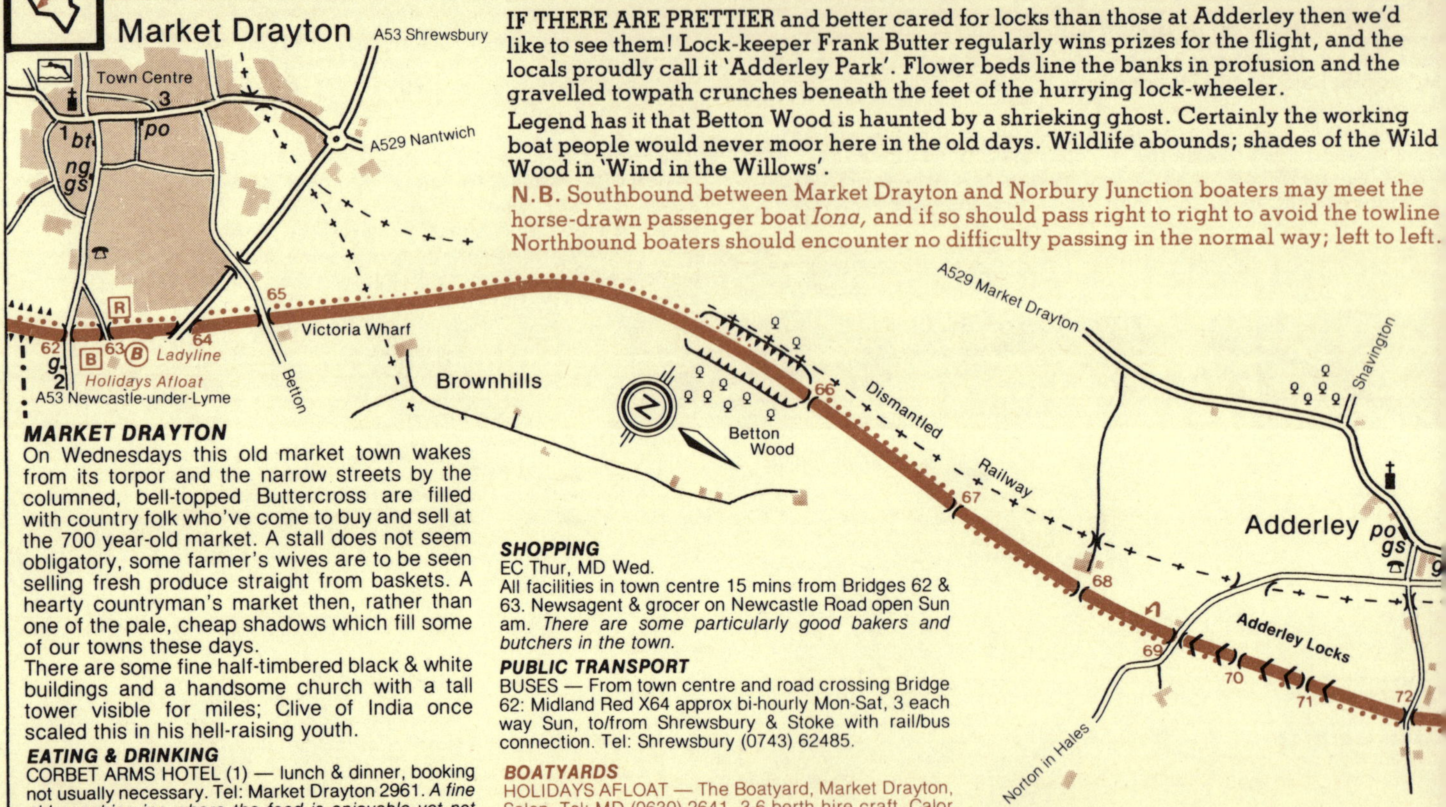

MARKET DRAYTON

On Wednesdays this old market town wakes from its torpor and the narrow streets by the columned, bell-topped Buttercross are filled with country folk who've come to buy and sell at the 700 year-old market. A stall does not seem obligatory, some farmer's wives are to be seen selling fresh produce straight from baskets. A hearty countryman's market then, rather than one of the pale, cheap shadows which fill some of our towns these days.

There are some fine half-timbered black & white buildings and a handsome church with a tall tower visible for miles; Clive of India once scaled this in his hell-raising youth.

EATING & DRINKING

CORBET ARMS HOTEL (1) — lunch & dinner, booking not usually necessary. Tel: Market Drayton 2961. *A fine old coaching inn where the food is enjoyable yet not over expensive.*

THE TALBOT (2) — Ansells & lunches.

THE RAILWAY (3) — Marstons, food & accommodation.

Numerous other pubs in town centre to suit all tastes.

SHOPPING

EC Thur, MD Wed.

All facilities in town centre 15 mins from Bridges 62 & 63. Newsagent & grocer on Newcastle Road open Sun am. *There are some particularly good bakers and butchers in the town.*

PUBLIC TRANSPORT

BUSES — From town centre and road crossing Bridge 62: Midland Red X64 approx bi-hourly Mon-Sat, 3 each way Sun, to/from Shrewsbury & Stoke with rail/bus connection. Tel: Shrewsbury (0743) 62485.

BOATYARDS

HOLIDAYS AFLOAT — The Boatyard, Market Drayton, Salop. Tel: MD (0630) 2641. 3-6 berth hire craft. Calor gas, chandlery & canalia.

LADYLINE — Bank Chambers, 3 Cheshire Street, Market Drayton. Tel: MD 3101. Water, Calor gas, petrol, moorings, slipway, boat sales & brokerage, chandlery & leisure wear.

ADDERLEY

SHOPPING

Post office stores open daily, 10 mins walk from Bridge 72.

9 SHROPSHIRE UNION CANAL — 30mls/13½hrs Autherley Jnct — Barbridge Jnct 8mls/4hrs

FIFTEEN LOCKS RUNNING THROUGH a breezy cutting of larch and Scots pine take the canal from Shropshire to Cheshire or vice versa, raising or lowering the canal to the tune of almost 100 feet. Like those at Adderley they are well maintained and a pleasure to operate. Between Locks 12 & 13 you pass Audlem Wharf, one of the prettiest ports of call on the FOUR COUNTIES RING.

Near the bottom lock the 'Shroppie' bounds across the little river Weaver upon a high embankment. An equal bound in our imagination is required to credit the story that during the last war there was talk of making this shallow stream navigable, joining it to the Shropshire Union at this point by a barge lift on the same principal as that at Anderton, and replacing the flights of locks at Audlem, Adderley and Tryley with similar machinery, so that 100 ton capacity barges could trade between Merseyside and the Midlands. Today's pleasure boater can be thankful that the plan never materialised, but there are those of us who have a sneaking belief that canals, properly invested in, could carry much of the heavy freight monopolised by the road lobby.

NB. Boaters should proceed slowly with caution between Locks 12 & 13 past the busy wharf at Audlem. Note also that you can moor both sides at this point, but for no longer than 24 hours.

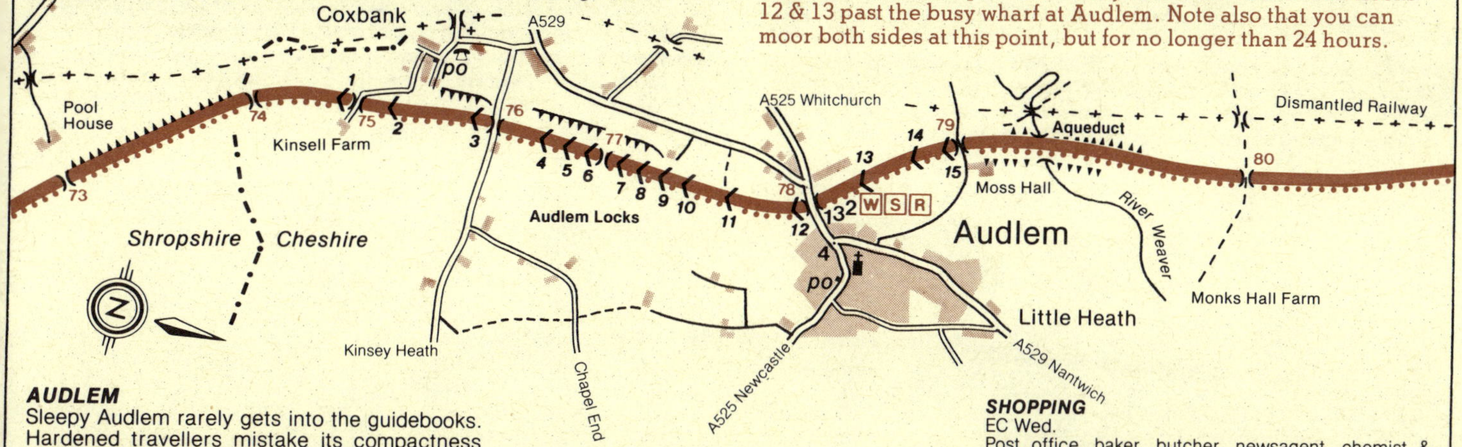

AUDLEM

Sleepy Audlem rarely gets into the guidebooks. Hardened travellers mistake its compactness for a lack of character, and have driven through it before they have time to fall for its mix of redbrick and timber buildings lying at the feet of the noble parish church of St James the Great. The Crosville bus to Crewe departs from what must be the prettiest bus shelter in England, an old oak-beamed, stone-pillared market cross. If you miss Audlem you might just as well have stayed at home with the TV!

EATING & DRINKING

BRIDGE INN (1) — Marstons, sandwiches, pool & darts.
THE SHROPPIE FLY (2) — Free house, snacks, lunches, teas & dinners; children's room. *Canally atmosphere.*
More pubs in centre.

SHOPPING

EC Wed.
Post office, baker, butcher, newsagent, chemist & general stores. Nat West (Mon & Thur 10-12.30) Barclays (Tue & Thur 10-2.30) banks.
AUDLEM MILL CANAL SHOP (3) — Once a busy canal-side mill but now one of the best canal craft shops in the country. Not to be missed.

PUBLIC TRANSPORT

BUSES — From Market Cross (4): Crosville K41/K61 approx bi-hourly Mon-Fri, 4 each way on Sat, no Sun, to/from Nantwich & Crewe, rail/bus connections at both points. Tel: Crewe (0270) 212256.

THERE'S A BRACE OF LOCKS at Hack Green, where part of the old stable block survives from the time when all the working boats were horse-drawn, and it was customary to change horses for the fast 'fly' boats which travelled day and night.
The canal runs straight as a well struck cover drive across the Cheshire Plain. Dairy farming has long been a vital part of the economy of this region. We tend to think of farming as an unchanging facet of the landscape, but the black & white Fresian cattle, now so synonymous with Cheshire, are a relatively recent introduction. The working boatman of the last century would not recognise these black & white interlopers from the Low Countries. When he passed this way the fields would have been filled with indigenous breeds such as Ayrshires and Alderneys.
There have been other changes too. One of the two railways which cross this table top countryside has closed. It used to carry copper-capped Great Western Railway engines hauling carriages coloured chocolate and cream, on their way to Wellington and Crewe. But the last train passed this way 15 years ago, and the rails have long since been lifted. The other railway — Crewe to Cardiff — continues to flourish; a useful cross-country link along the Welsh Marches.
The Birmingham & Liverpool Junction Canal was opened between Nantwich and Autherley in 1835 — the last major canal (other than the Manchester Ship Canal which was in a different league altogether!) to be built. But by the time it was opened Britain had been overtaken by the Railway Age, and narrowboats carrying 25 tons at 3mph could hardly compete with goods trains steaming along at 25mph with a payload in the hundreds of tons. Nevertheless, after it was taken over by the London & North Western Railway in 1846, the canal continued to be heavily used, largely because it penetrated deep into rival Great Western Railway territory, and there was a great deal of competition for cargoes.

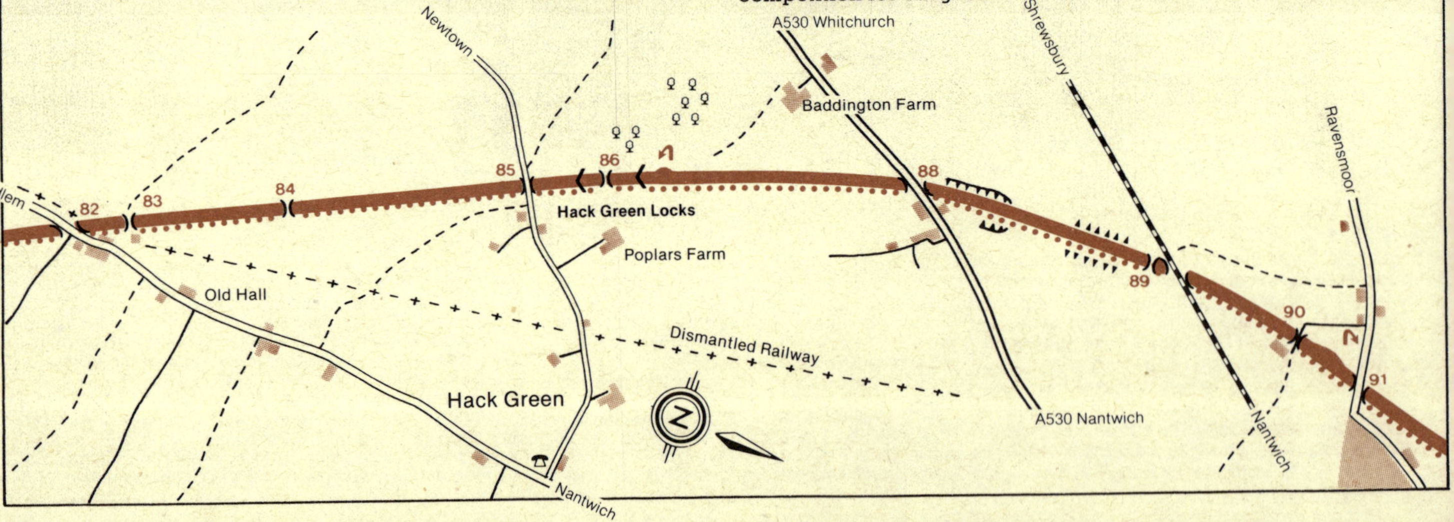

Norbury Junction

A visit to
CHURCHE'S MANSION

Churche's Mansion was built by Thomas Clease, carpenter, for Richard & Margerye Churche. Completed on Saturday the 4th of May 1577, it remains very true to its original construction and design, which reflects the life style and success of Richard Churche, who in his life so prospered, as to become one of the fifty wealthiest gentlemen in Cheshire, who were persuaded to contribute to the defence of the realm against the Armada. His portion was £25!

The mansion, moated and North facing, is of an 'H' plan framed in oak with daubed and plastered infilling. The timber required for the building was felled some eight miles distant, confirming the town's age, prosperity and industry of boiling brine, which had consumed good building timber within this radius. To reduce the weight of timber transported, the carpenter Thomas Clease took his plans to the forest, cut and sized his timbers, and numbered them for re-assembly on site in Hospital Street. His carpenters marks are still evident and are in two styles. The exterior joints have matching Arabic numerals carved on either side of a joint, whilst the joints on the timbers within the building hidden in the principal rooms by ceilings and panelling, have scribed Roman numerals.

Richard Churche achieved his wealth for the building of the mansion (when he was thirty seven years old) by the purchase and leasing of land and property. When he died fifteen years later his land interests stretched from Stafford to Middlewich, and he bequeathed to his elder son William an estate at Beton in Shropshire, his second son Randle succeeding to the mansion and the care of his widowed mother Margerye. Though the mansion may have been the second son's portion, it was very dear to Richard, who requested in his will that the mansion should always bear his name and entailed it to his male issue.

Cheshire Life

It is curious that a gentleman and land owner should choose to build and live within his native town subject to noisome smells, disease and fire. This choice and the feudal design of the mansion (to accommodate some eight or ten male servants) suggests that there was more to fear from pony mounted bands of thieves and robbers from across the Welsh Border.

For the mansion to have survived these past four hundred years as a one date construction, stripped of later modernisations, is a remarkable piece of good fortune, and enables the visitor to see a complete home of 1577. The mansion cannot be maintained or further restored on the income from visitors. The owners therefore use the ground floor as a licensed restaurant open throughout the year, and the first floor is furnished in oak as a visual aid to the viewer of the mansion from April to October.

Admission to view Churche's Mansion from April to October costs 40p adults and 20p children. However, by showing your copy of this CANAL COMPANION on entry, one adult or two children will be admitted free of charge.

Churche's Mansion restaurant is open daily throughout the year for morning coffee, lunch and dinner (except Sunday evening). Tel: Nantwich (0270) 625933 for bookings. When the mansion is open to view light refreshments are available during the afternoon.

11 SHROPSHIRE UNION CANAL 38mls/17½hrs Autherley Jnct — Barbridge Jnct 2mls/½hrs

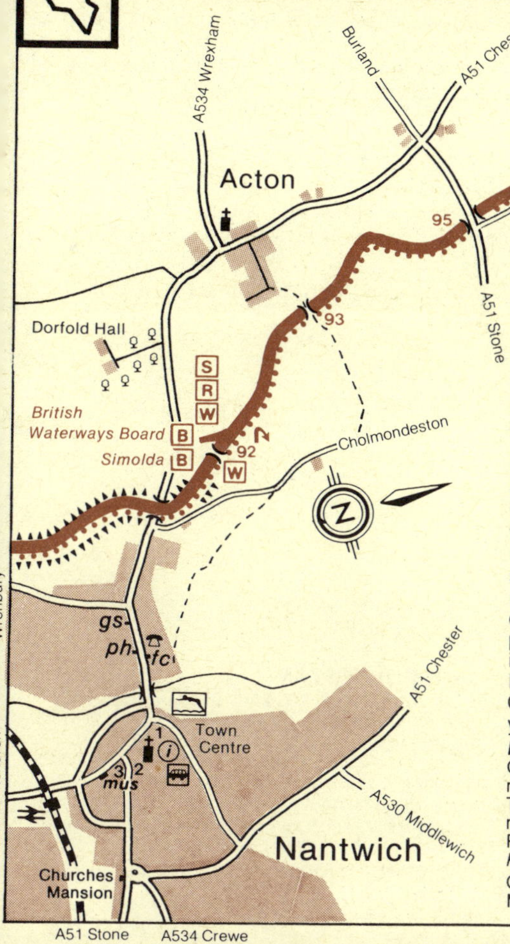

A BROAD EMBANKMENT carries the canal high above the allotments and back gardens on the western outskirts of Nantwich, crossing the Chester road upon a fine cast iron aqueduct by Telford. In case of a leakage in the embankment there are stop gates at either end so that the section can be sealed off if necessary. Oddly enough the embankment need not have been built at all, had the owners of nearby Dorfold Hall not objected to the passage of the canal across their land. The busy basin and former terminus of the Chester Canal (opened in 1779) suggests the route that would have been taken. The character of the Shropshire Union changes at this point. Northbound are the broad but winding waters of its earlier constituent the Chester Canal. Southbound the direct but narrow former Birmingham & Liverpool Junction Canal.

NANTWICH

The octagonal tower of St Mary's, seen across the rooftops from the canal embankment, tempts you to moor awhile and make friends with this Cheshire market town — one of England's lovelist. It's 15 minutes walk to the centre; though shops and pubs can be found on the way in if you're in a hurry. But do try to go all the way, over the stone bridge that spans the river Weaver, and into the narrow winding streets of half timbered buildings. An inner ring-road has lately taken much of the road traffic out of the centre, which makes Nantwich a jolly place to walk about in. You can purchase an inexpensive booklet — "Walkabout Tour of Nantwich" — from the Tourist Information Centre which gives you all the facts; if it's facts you want to know!

EATING & DRINKING

OAT MARKET COFFEE HOUSE (1) — Coffees, light meals, teas. *Nice beamy 1st-floor cafe.*

THE LAMB (2) — Bar meals Mon-Sat or restaurant meals (ex Sun evening). *Solid, old-school hotel.*

PADDLES (3) — Hamburgers, grills, steaks etc. *Was Kepple's, still lots of fun.*

ODDFELLOWS ARMS — Ansells, lunchtime bar food Mon-Sat. Nearest pub to canal.

SHOPPING

EC Wed, MD Thur & Sat.

All facilities in town centre. Nantwich is a first-class shopping centre with particularly good foodshops; butchers, bakers, and cheese sellers.

PUBLIC TRANSPORT

BUSES — From bus station. Frequent Crosville services to all parts of NW. Tel: Crewe (0270) 212256.

TRAINS — Station 20 mins from canal. Approx 10 trains each way Mon-Sat between Crewe & Shrewsbury with good connections. Trains also call at Wrenbury & Whitchurch on Llangollen Canal. No Sunday service. Tel: Crewe (0270) 55245.

PLACES TO VISIT

TOURIST INFORMATION CENTRE — Located by bus station in Beam Street. Tel: Nantwich 623914.

DORFOLD HALL — ¼m W of canal basin. Open Tues & Bank Hol Mons Apr-Oct; admission £1 adults, 50p children. Jacobean house dating from 1616, beautiful gardens. Tel: Nantwich 625245.

CHURCHES MANSION — see opposite.

NANTWICH MUSEUM — always seems to be closed!

BOATYARDS

BRITISH WATERWAYS BOARD — Chester Road, Nantwich, Cheshire. Tel: Nantwich (0270) 625122. 4 to 8 berth hire craft. Pumpout, Elsan disposal, water, Calor gas, rubbish disposal, drydock, canalia.

SIMOLDA — Basin End, Nantwich, Cheshire. Tel: Nantwich 624075. 6 to 8 berth hire craft.

REMOTE AND SEEMINGLY always windswept, the Middlewich Branch of the Shropshire Union Canal cuts across the grain of the landscape on a series of high embankments. It can be a very busy length of canal, there is an extensive marina at Cholmondeston and the branch is a vital link in the North-west's inland waterway system, funnelling traffic towards the popular Llangollen Canal.

Historically, the branch, opened in 1833, belonged to the Chester Canal Company and was engineered by — you've guessed it, Thomas Telford! Trade was heavy in cargo-carrying days too. In 1888 an attempt was made to replace horse haulage by running a narrow-gauge railway along the towing path, and employing steam locomotives to pull strings of narrowboats. But this system of haulage proved impractical, though it did catch on abroad, particularly on the French waterways.

NB. The locks on the Middlewich Branch are deep and heavy-gated. Send your strongest crew members ahead to work them!

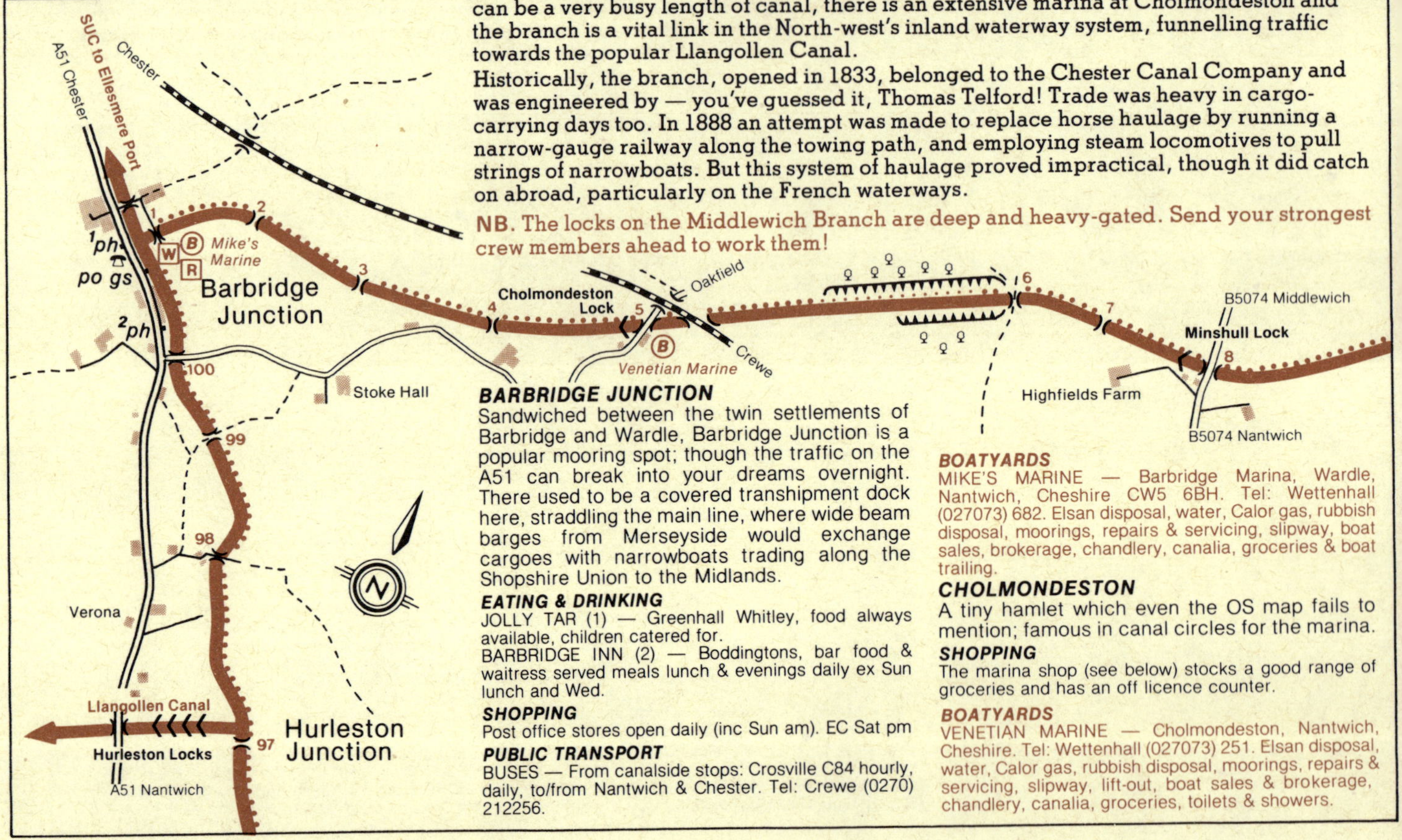

BARBRIDGE JUNCTION

Sandwiched between the twin settlements of Barbridge and Wardle, Barbridge Junction is a popular mooring spot; though the traffic on the A51 can break into your dreams overnight. There used to be a covered transhipment dock here, straddling the main line, where wide beam barges from Merseyside would exchange cargoes with narrowboats trading along the Shopshire Union to the Midlands.

EATING & DRINKING

JOLLY TAR (1) — Greenhall Whitley, food always available, children catered for.

BARBRIDGE INN (2) — Boddingtons, bar food & waitress served meals lunch & evenings daily ex Sun lunch and Wed.

SHOPPING

Post office stores open daily (inc Sun am). EC Sat pm

PUBLIC TRANSPORT

BUSES — From canalside stops: Crosville C84 hourly, daily, to/from Nantwich & Chester. Tel: Crewe (0270) 212256.

BOATYARDS

MIKE'S MARINE — Barbridge Marina, Wardle, Nantwich, Cheshire CW5 6BH. Tel: Wettenhall (027073) 682. Elsan disposal, water, Calor gas, rubbish disposal, moorings, repairs & servicing, slipway, boat sales, brokerage, chandlery, canalia, groceries & boat trailing.

CHOLMONDESTON

A tiny hamlet which even the OS map fails to mention; famous in canal circles for the marina.

SHOPPING

The marina shop (see below) stocks a good range of groceries and has an off licence counter.

BOATYARDS

VENETIAN MARINE — Cholmondeston, Nantwich, Cheshire. Tel: Wettenhall (027073) 251. Elsan disposal, water, Calor gas, rubbish disposal, moorings, repairs & servicing, slipway, lift-out, boat sales & brokerage, chandlery, canalia, groceries, toilets & showers.

Nature Book

The Heron

IN SPITE of being really rather common on the inland waterways the Grey Heron, *Ardea cinerea*, is still an impressive enough sight to draw most boaters out of the comforts of the cabin for a better view. One would almost think the bird was playing some peculiar game of Grandmother's Footsteps as it tantalises the observer; waiting until the boat is just beyond the verge of focal range before picking its lethargic way up into the air and easing itself fifty yards or so further down the canal. There it will remain, a grey dash on the canal bank, until the boat is close enough again for the game to be repeated. Seeming to tire of the activity after the third or fourth encounter the heron then circles back over treetops and open fields until out of sight around the last bend.

TWO things motivate this behaviour: Naturally enough the bird is wary of something as large and as noisy as a boat, so it will move away whenever the potential danger threatens. But because the boat comes from one direction the heron will fly off in the other and since the bird has strict feeding territories to adhere to it will eventually arrive at the limit of its patch. To avoid a confrontation with its neighbour it will be forced to leave the canal and fly back to some other, trouble free, part of its territory. I have seen individuals pressed too far and overstep the mark. With a flash of grey and black an irate and possessive neighbour tears into the attack and some quite alarming aerial battles can ensue.

THIS animosity is all the more curious when one considers that the birds are communal between March and August when they gather together in large colonies, or Heronries, to breed. The female lays from three to five eggs which the two birds incubate in turns. After 25 days the young hatch out and start demanding food. They stay in the nest for about two months, both adults sharing the responsibilities of rearing the young, until ready to fly.

AN ADULT Grey Heron is distinguishable from a juvenile by its long black head plumes. During the breeding season the normally yellow beak changes to a bright orange and this is used in conjunction with the plumes as part of the impressive courtship displays which take place in the treetops. A young heron will take several years to reach maturity.

THOUGH hounded down as poachers and thieves around fisheries and the like they suffer no such persecution on the canals and possibly because of this seem to be thriving.

Marcus Potts

13 SUC MIDDLEWICH BRANCH

4mls/1½hrs Barbridge Jnct — Middlewich 3mls/1½hrs

A RUMBUSTIOUS LENGTH OF CANAL carrying you loftily above the winding valley of the river Weaver, and giving expansive views towards a horizon bounded by Delamere Forest and the Peckforton Hills. Church Minshull, with its russet coloured brick and black & white timbering, looks like a toy village. Down there, somewhere, glimpsed through the woods, is a big expanse of water called Top Flash, a subsidence induced lake right beside the Weaver, a river which becomes navigable only a stone's throw downstream at Winsford; indeed, sea-going vessels use it regularly as far inland as Northwich.

Well to do farms border the canal, and their fields are either filled with big milking herds of Fresian cows whose numbers are stamped on their muddy bottoms, or cut red by the plough. The main London-Glasgow railway crosses the canal and its electric trains richocet by at thirty times your speed. To the South-east, just beyond the edge of the map, there's an older transport route, the Roman road linking the Roman salt mines at Nantwich and Middlewich.

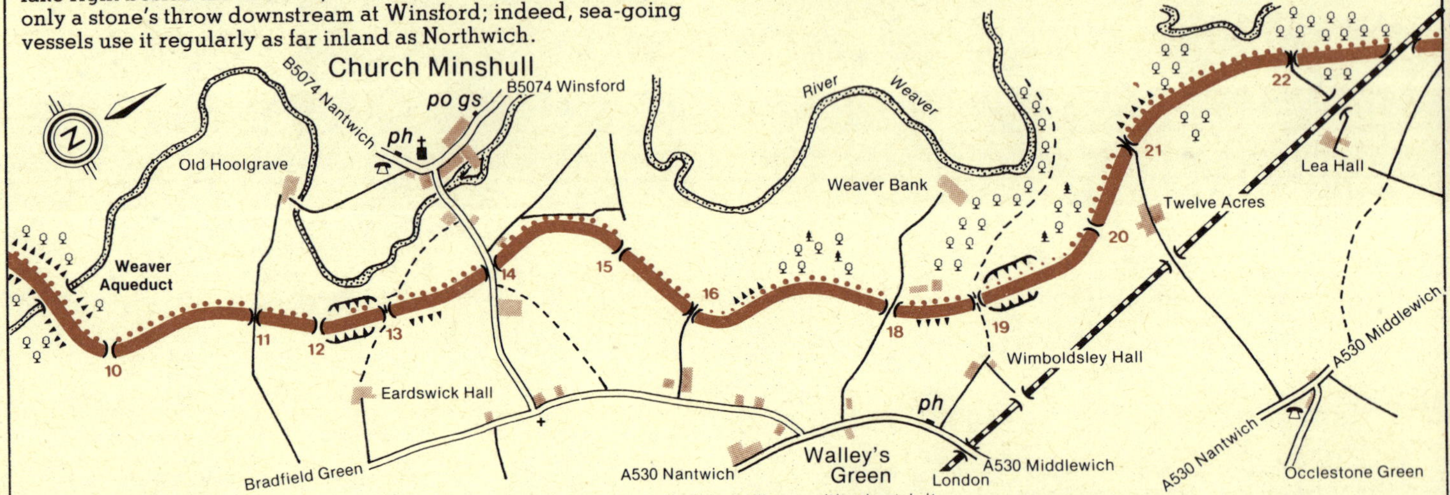

CHURCH MINSHULL

A pretty village of black & white cottages. Readers of L.T.C. Rolt's "Narrow Boat" — was he the first to cruise The Ring? — will recognise this as the place where the Rolts enjoyed an extended stay during the fateful Autumn of 1939. Rolt revelled in the close-knit community that flourished here — the blacksmith who shod the local cart horses, and the miller whose water wheel supplied the village with electricity (he continued to do so until 1960!). But the 'tide of black tarmacadam' which had only just covered the cobble sets of the main street brought many changes which would have broken Rolt's heart. Not surprisingly the smithy and mill are long silent, nevertheless, Church Minshull is worth the walk down from the canal, if only to reach the convivial bar of The Badger.

EATING & DRINKING

THE BADGER — Ind Coope & basket meals; garden. 10 mins walk from Bridge 14.

SHOPPING

Post office stores.

PUBLIC TRANSPORT

BUSES — From village centre: Crosville K31, hourly to/from Crewe & Northwich. Tel: Crewe (0270) 212256.

DOING THE RING you only really graze the outskirts of Middlewich, quickly moving out again into open country. Whether it be the long climb up out of Cheshire to the Potteries if you're going clockwise, or the roly-poly Cheshire dairy country if you're moving the other way.

NB . Care should be taken cruising the tight corner between Wardle and King's Locks, particularly when coming out of Wardle Lock beneath the road bridge as your view is restricted, and boats often congregate to use the water point on the towpath side at the foot of King's Lock.

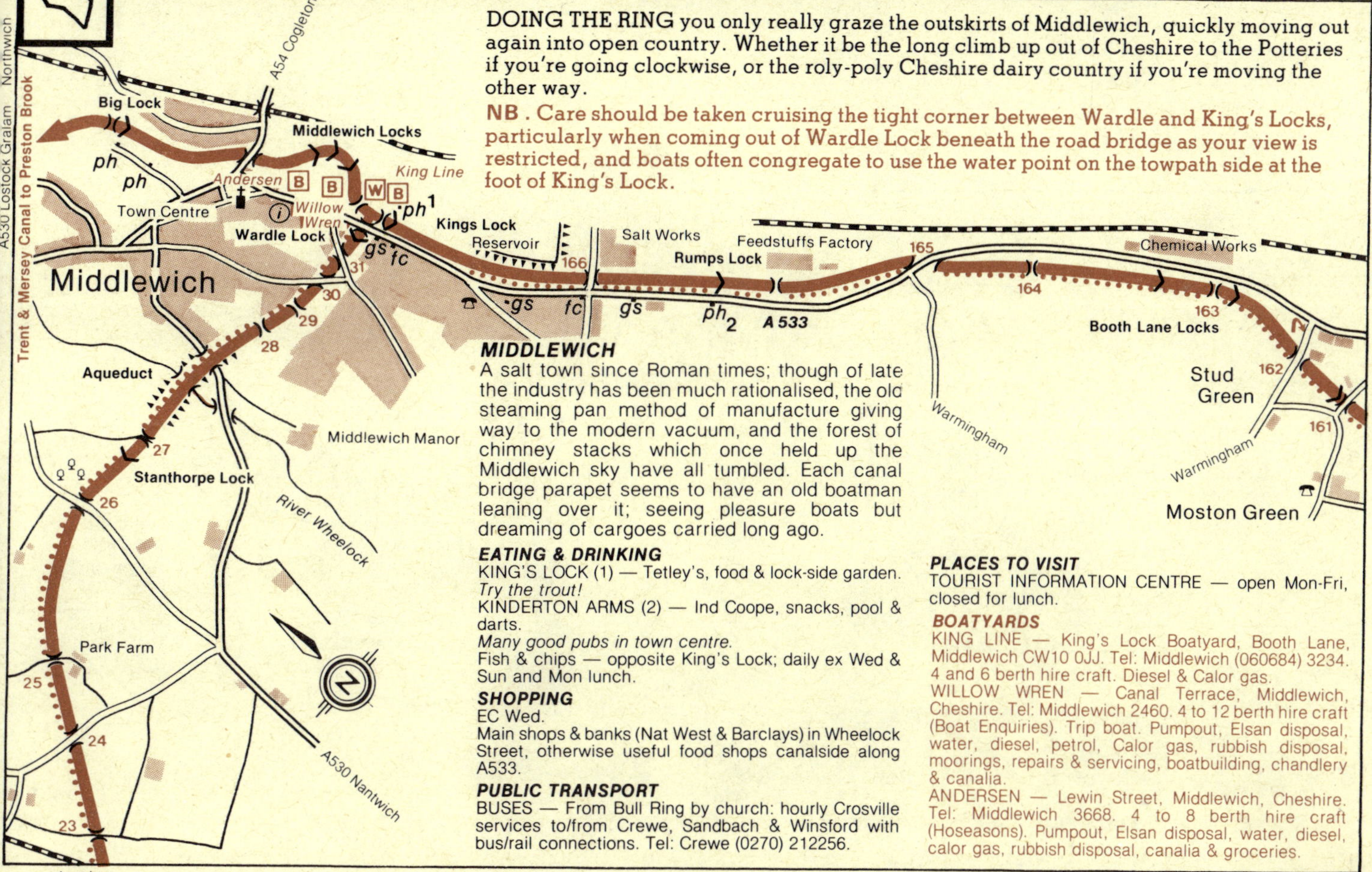

MIDDLEWICH

A salt town since Roman times; though of late the industry has been much rationalised, the old steaming pan method of manufacture giving way to the modern vacuum, and the forest of chimney stacks which once held up the Middlewich sky have all tumbled. Each canal bridge parapet seems to have an old boatman leaning over it; seeing pleasure boats but dreaming of cargoes carried long ago.

EATING & DRINKING

KING'S LOCK (1) — Tetley's, food & lock-side garden. *Try the trout!*

KINDERTON ARMS (2) — Ind Coope, snacks, pool & darts.

Many good pubs in town centre.

Fish & chips — opposite King's Lock; daily ex Wed & Sun and Mon lunch.

SHOPPING

EC Wed.

Main shops & banks (Nat West & Barclays) in Wheelock Street, otherwise useful food shops canalside along A533.

PUBLIC TRANSPORT

BUSES — From Bull Ring by church: hourly Crosville services to/from Crewe, Sandbach & Winsford with bus/rail connections. Tel: Crewe (0270) 212256.

PLACES TO VISIT

TOURIST INFORMATION CENTRE — open Mon-Fri, closed for lunch.

BOATYARDS

KING LINE — King's Lock Boatyard, Booth Lane, Middlewich CW10 0JJ. Tel: Middlewich (060684) 3234. 4 and 6 berth hire craft. Diesel & Calor gas.

WILLOW WREN — Canal Terrace, Middlewich, Cheshire. Tel: Middlewich 2460. 4 to 12 berth hire craft (Boat Enquiries). Trip boat. Pumpout, Elsan disposal, water, diesel, petrol, Calor gas, rubbish disposal, moorings, repairs & servicing, boatbuilding, chandlery & canalia.

ANDERSEN — Lewin Street, Middlewich, Cheshire. Tel: Middlewich 3668. 4 to 8 berth hire craft (Hoseasons). Pumpout, Elsan disposal, water, diesel, calor gas, rubbish disposal, canalia & groceries.

The FOUR COUNTIES Ring
Woodseaves High Bridge
Autherley Junction
Brewood Speedwell castle
Stone
Joules Brewer
Gailey Roundhouse
Railway Station
Great Haywood Essex Bridge
Sandon War Memorial

Nantwich
Tollmache Almshouses
Audlem Mill
Buttermarket
Church Minshull St. Bartholemew's
Stoke
Potbank
Hassall Green
Mission
Church
Heartbreak Hill

THE CANAL TRAVERSES an austere region of abandoned salt workings. Subsidence is a perennial problem, and thus the canal banks are constructed of steel piles embedded in concrete. Little remains of the once numerous salt works. Only the cold base of a chimney stack or the gaunt shell of an engine house points to the scene of former brine pumping or rock salt cutting. But in the past salt cargoes were carried by water from hereabouts to the Mersey ports for export, and narrowboats brought in coal from North Staffordshire pits to fire the open steaming pans where brine was evaporated leaving salt deposits.

NB 1. Subsidence has rendered the canal very deep in places. Non-swimmers should be life-jacketed.

NB 2. Southbound the Wheelock flight of locks begins. Those marked 'd' are duplicated, ie there are two chambers side by side. You may use either chamber in either direction.

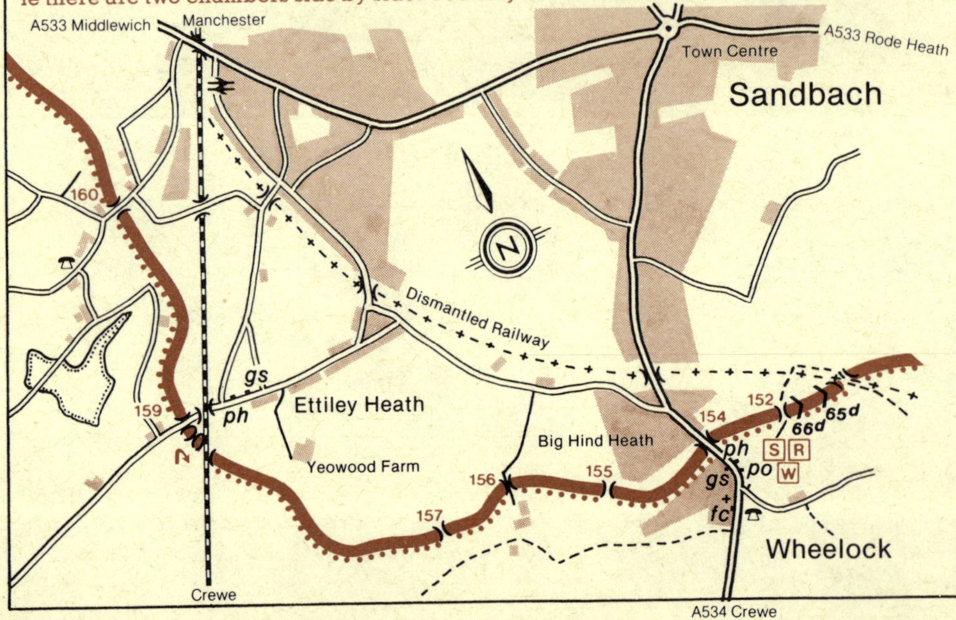

SANDBACH

Famous for the Saxon crosses to be found in the cobbled market place. All services available. EC Tue, MD Thur. Town centre 1½ miles from canal at Wheelock (see Buses).

Sandbach Crosses

WHEELOCK

Old warehouses still line the canal at this useful suburb of Sandbach; a good spot to take on water and replenish the galley after or before tackling the long flight of locks to and from Kidsgrove.

EATING & DRINKING

CHESHIRE CHEESE — Ansells & pub grub; canalside. *Two other pubs as well.*

Fish & chips — Tue-Sat lunch & evening + Thur & Fri tea-times. Eat in or take out. *Humourous owner!*

SHOPPING

Post office, 2 general stores, newsagent, butcher (ng & gs open Sun am).

PUBLIC TRANSPORT

BUSES — Crosville K33-7, half-hourly weekdays, hourly Sundays to/from Crewe, Sandbach & Middlewich. Tel: Crewe (0270) 212256.

TRAINS — Sandbach station, ½m NE of Bridge 160; local trains to/from Manchester & Crewe. Tel: Crewe (0270) 55245.

LOCKS, LOCKS, AND MORE LOCKS — hard work for the boater whichever way you're going. This long climb or descent is nicknamed 'Heartbreak Hill' for good reason! Most of these locks were duplicated in the 1830's to speed up traffic in the face of railway competition, and, of course, they still ease delays to this day, as well as giving you a chance to swap travellers' tales with those working through the adjacent chamber.

At Thurlwood you'll find one of the most unusual locks on the inland waterways. In appearance it resembles a giant weighing machine. Made of steel, it was opened in 1958 to combat subsidence. The theory was that the tank or chamber could be raised in compensation. But, in practice, the lock has spent long periods out of commission, and even when it has been in use, operation is so complicated that most prefer to work through the adjacent conventional lock.

NB. Duplicated locks — Those shown 'd' on the maps have two separate chambers, side by side. Boats can use either chamber in either direction, though it's naturally easier to use those that are set in your direction. Operation is exactly the same as for other locks. Note, though, that occasionally a chamber may be closed for repairs.

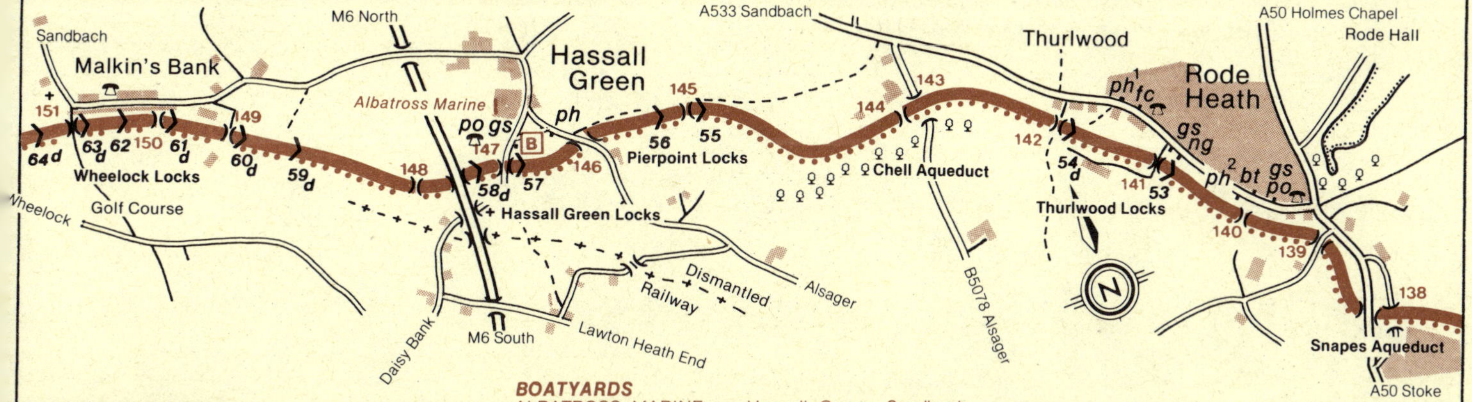

HASSALL GREEN

A good place for a breather. Surprisingly the M6 does not over intrude. Nice walk down the lane to the pretty pink mission church.

EATING & DRINKING

THE ROMPING DONKEY — Ind Coope, bar food & restaurant meals; garden.

SHOPPING

Post office stores open daily. Good canal craft shop offering lockside coffees and teas.

BOATYARDS

ALBATROSS MARINE — Hassall Green, Sandbach CW11 0YB. Tel: Sandbach (09367) 2266. 4 & 6 berth hire craft.

VISTRA MARINA — as above. Pumpout, water, diesel, paraffin, Calor gas, moorings, chandlery & canal shop.

RODE HEATH & THURLWOOD

EATING & DRINKING

ROYAL OAK (1) — Ind Coope, lunches Mon-Sat, basket meals in evening daily. Table skittles. Live entertainment Wed, Sat & Sun.

BROUGHTON ARMS (2) — Marstons, food Mon-Fri lunch, sandwiches at other times.

Fish & chips — Tue-Sat lunch & evening.

SHOPPING

Post office stores, butcher & newsagent.

PUBLIC TRANSPORT

BUSES — From stops on A533, Potteries Motor Traction. Timetable changing radically as we went to press, telephone Stoke (0782) 48811 for details.

17 TRENT & MERSEY CANAL 10mls/7hrs Middlewich — Great Haywood 22mls/9½hrs

AT HARDING'S WOOD JUNCTION the Macclesfield Canal, part of the popular 'Cheshire Ring', heads misleadingly and disconcertingly off in a South-easterly direction before doubling back to cross the Trent & Mersey by aqueduct.

The Trent & Mersey Canal pierces the gritstone wedge of Harecastle Hill by way of a 1¾ mile tunnel built by Thomas Telford (and several hundred others!) in 1827. At either end you can see the abandoned portals of an earlier tunnel by Brindley, dating from 1777 and the opening of the Trent & Mersey. Boats had to be propelled through the original tunnel by 'leggers' lying on their backs and literally walking a boat from one end to the other, a feat which took 3 hours! Moreover, there was no room inside for boats to pass and the tunnel was a serious bottleneck.

To alleviate delays a second tunnel was commissioned with Telford in charge. Provision of a towpath, and later an electric-powered tug, significantly speeded traffic, though, the company rejected plans to enlarge Brindley's tunnel. The later was used side by side with the new tunnel until after the First World War, when traffic was concentrated on Telford's tunnel, the latter surviving into the pleasure boating era, albeit having been closed for 4 years during the 1970s after roof falls caused by subsidence. Nowadays you go through under your own steam and engine fumes are sucked out by a giant extractor fan at the South end.

NB 1. The single-lane Harecastle tunnel operates to a timetable of entry times; see page 48.

NB 2. Locks marked 'd' are duplicated; either chamber may be used in either direction.

EATING & DRINKING

RED BULL — Robinson's & bar meals. Canalside Lock 43.

THE TAVERN — Ind Coope & bar meals. Canalside Lock 41.

THE BLUE BELL — Younger's & pub grub. Canalside Lock 41.

SHOPPING

Kidsgrove shops are dull, for emergency use only!

PUBLIC TRANSPORT

BUSES — Potteries Motor Traction. Tel: Stoke (0782) 48811.

TRAINS — Frequent trains daily to/from Stoke, Crewe, Manchester & Derby. Tel: Stoke (0782) 411411. *The train service is useful if you're walking the towpath (which doesn't go through the tunnel anymore) or if you have crew members that suffer from claustrophobia. Book to Longport station on the far side of the tunnel, 5 mins walk from Longport Wharf.*

BOATYARDS

DAVID PIPER — Red Bull Basin, Church Lawton, Stoke-on-Trent. Tel: Kidsgrove (07816) 4754. Pumpout, water, diesel, calor gas, moorings, repairs & servicing, slipway, crane, boatbuilding, sales & brokerage, chandlery & canalia; payphone.

KIDSGROVE

A one-time colliery town on the Cheshire/Staffordshire border, remarkable only for the fact that for all his genius, James Brindley lies in an obscure chapel cemetery in the suburb of Newchapel.

18 TRENT & MERSEY CANAL 15mls/9½hrs Middlewich — Great Haywood 17mls/8½hrs

THE TRENT & MERSEY CANAL plunges through the heart of the Potteries, its *raison d'etre*. But it's a heart that has suffered an appalling coronary in recent years. Josiah Wedgwood's Etruria factory was swept away as long ago as 1968; in the once torrid and pandemonic crucible of Shelton Bar the rolling mill tolls like a death knell; cranes hang quite hopelessly over pottery wharves where boats once queued to discharge their milky coloured cargoes of china clay and felspar; and the furnaces and offices that were Goldendale Ironworks have crumbled into wasteland. The only winners are Industrial archaeologists who will have a field day deciphering clues from a busier past. A bottle kiln survives by Bridge 126 at Longport; there's a six storey flour mill at Middleport; the blue brick offices of Shelton Steelworks were once Josiah Wedgwood's Etruria residence; an enigmatic roundhouse by Bridge 118 is all that remains of the Etruria pottery; but there is life after death for the Etruscan Bone Mill by Lock 39 for there are plans to open a museum here.

Five of the six pottery towns — Tunstall, Burslem, Hanley, Fenton and Longton lie along the ridge to the East of the canal; only Stoke stands down at canal level. In these amorphous yet fiercely independant towns they used to proudly sell postcards of the smoke that billowed from ovens and chimnies, because smoke, dirt and grime spelt prosperity. Writers have been fascinated by the region. Wells, Orwell and Priestley have all vividly recounted their visits here, but it is indisputably Arnold Bennett country, and cruising along the 'Knype & Mersey Canal' which opens 'Clayhanger', it's nice to muse that there are still Darius Clayhangers, Anna Tellwrights and above all Denry Machins to be found somewhere up in that black brick maze.

NB. The bridges on this section have reduced headroom. Keep off the cabin roof and watch your head.

NB Built up areas not shown in detail to aid clarity

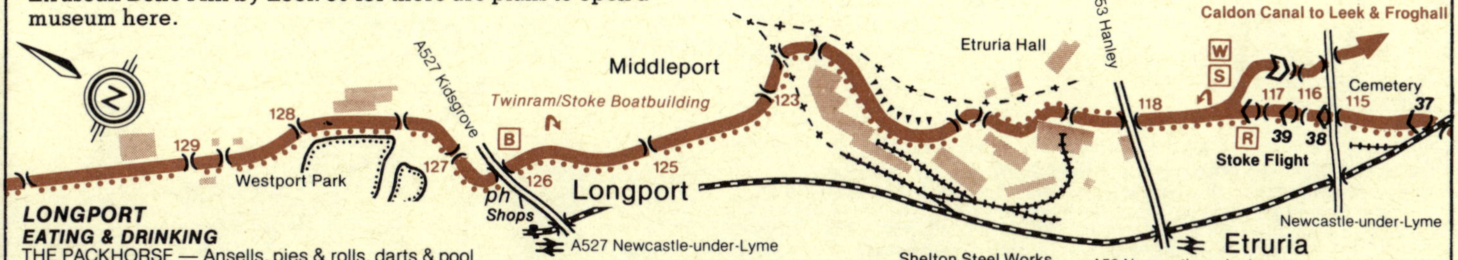

LONGPORT

EATING & DRINKING

THE PACKHORSE — Ansells, pies & rolls, darts & pool.
DUKE OF BRIDGEWATER — Bass, pub grub and canalia.

SHOPPING

Post office, general stores, butcher, newsagent, fish & chips. The most handily place shops on your journey through the Potteries.

PUBLIC TRANSPORT

BUSES — Potteries Motor Traction. Tel: Stoke (0782) 48811.
TRAINS — ¼m W of Bridge 126. Frequent trains daily to/from Stoke, Crewe, Manchester & Derby. Tel: Stoke 411411. *The trains are useful if you wish to avoid towpathless Harecastle Tunnel or if any of your crew members suffer from claustrophobia. Book to Kidsgrove station canalside at the other end.*

BOATYARDS

TWINRAM — Longport Wharf, Station Street, Longport, Stoke ST6 4NA. Tel: Stoke (0782) 812674. 4 to 12 berth hire craft. Pumpout, Elsan disposal, water, diesel, Calor gas, rubbish disposal, short-term moorings, repairs & servicing, slipway, crane, boat sales & brokerage, chandlery & canalia.

STOKE-ON-TRENT BOATBUILDING CO — address as above. Tel: Stoke 813822. Steel boatbuilding, repairs & servicing, refits & repaints.

ETRURIA

Named after the ancient state of Italy by Josiah Wedgwood when he built his pottery works here in 1768. Junction of the Trent & Mersey and Caldon canals, the latter making a beautiful journey up into the Staffordshire moorlands.

19 TRENT & MERSEY CANAL 20mls/11½hrs Middlewich — Great Haywood 13mls/7hrs

THE CANAL TRAVELLER cannot help but feel cocooned. Partly by the concrete dominance of the Queensway road, partly by the canyon-like factory walls. But the canal seems to slip so easily through Stoke, that Southbound you're soon out into the open, if rather pock-marked country, whilst Northbound the gruelling pleasures of the Stoke flight of five claim your attention. The bottom lock has a deep concrete chamber, dating from the construction of the Queensway which necessitated partial slewing of the canal.

A blackened watercourse culverted beneath the canal is no less than the river Trent — would the mighty waterway that disgorges itself into the Humber 150 miles away admit to such humble origins?

Cruise through Stoke on a Saturday afternoon around 5 o'clock between September and May, and you may find the towpath and the bridges which cross the canal engulfed in a tide of grey, blue and brown reminiscent of that which begins J. B. Priestley's 'Good Companions'. The gait of the participants of this tide betrays that they have been to a football match, and you will cruise close by the red corrugated iron stands of the Victoria Ground where their dreams are fulfilled or battered once a winter fortnight when the 'Potters' play at home.

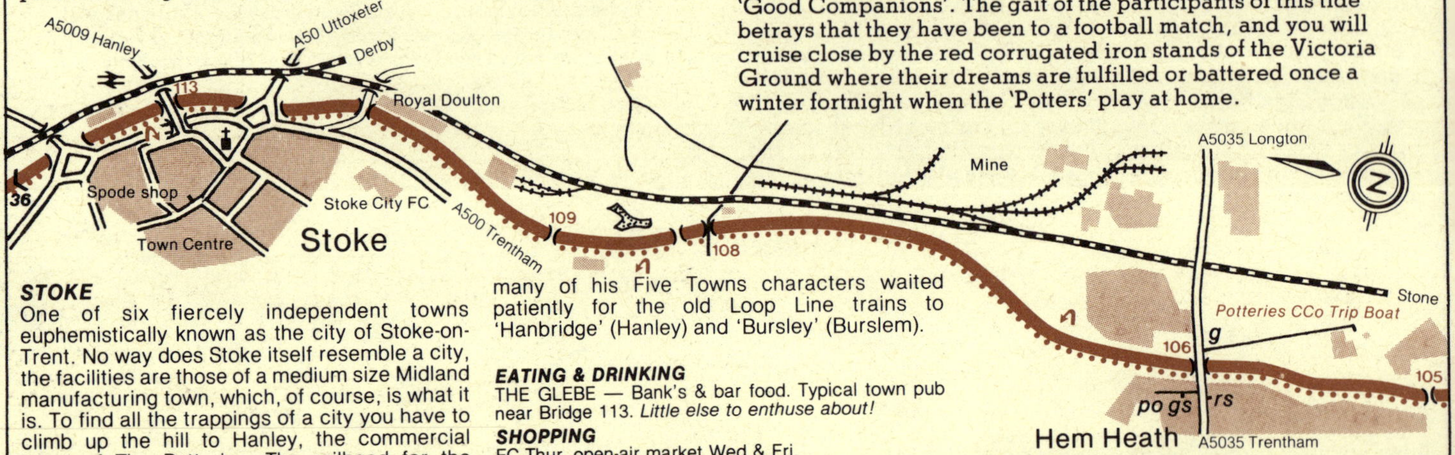

STOKE

One of six fiercely independent towns euphemistically known as the city of Stoke-on-Trent. No way does Stoke itself resemble a city, the facilities are those of a medium size Midland manufacturing town, which, of course, is what it is. To find all the trappings of a city you have to climb up the hill to Hanley, the commercial heart of The Potteries. The railhead for the district is here, though, behind that black retaining wall. Round the front, the station is a gem, a sort of Jacobean mansion with trail-filled platforms where you'd expect to find the ha-ha! A slightly bemused statue of Josiah Wedgwood looks on (he is also celebrated in the much restored parish church) — shouldn't he be looking at the canal? As 'Knype' in Arnold Bennett's stories, Stoke station was where many of his Five Towns characters waited patiently for the old Loop Line trains to 'Hanbridge' (Hanley) and 'Bursley' (Burslem).

EATING & DRINKING

THE GLEBE — Bank's & bar food. Typical town pub near Bridge 113. *Little else to enthuse about!*

SHOPPING

EC Thur, open-air market Wed & Fri. All facilities 5 mins from Bridge 113.

PUBLIC TRANSPORT

BUSES — Potteries Motor Traction. Radical timetable changes as we went to press. Tel: Stoke (0782) 48811 for latest details.

TRAINS — station canalside by Bridge 113. Major railhead. Tel: Stoke 411411.

PLACES TO VISIT

SPODE POTTERY — Tours by prior application — Tel: Stoke 46011 — but factory shop open to callers.

HEM HEATH

Suburb of Trentham. Good spot to moor overnight. Trips aboard traditional narrowboat *Flamingo*, Potteries Cruising Co. Tel: Stoke (0782) 657507.

EATING & DRINKING

TOBY INNS GRILL — Canalside by Bridge 106.

SHOPPING

Post office stores, open Sun am.

Harecastle Tunnel South

A visit to
WEDGWOOD VISITOR CENTRE

The story of Wedgwood began with the birth of Josiah Wedgwood in 1730 at Burslem, one of the pottery towns of North Staffordshire. Although his father was a potter, he was not a particularly successful one, and so Josiah was forced to make his own way. This he rapidly did, and by the time he was in his early twenties, he was already partner in a small but thriving pottery. In 1759 he started his own business, evolving a distinctive green glaze which became immensely popular, so much so that Wedgwood could soon count royalty amongst his customers. In 1769 he opened a new factory between Hanley and Newcastle-under-Lyme, and called it Etruria, after the ancient Italian state whose arts were influential at the time.

Recognising the need for improved transport — both for the import of raw materials and the export of finished goods — Wedgwood supported James Brindley in his plans to build a canal linking the rivers Mersey and Trent. That canal — the Trent & Mersey which we cruise today — opened in 1777 and it had an immediate impact on the Potteries, enabling Wedgwood pottery ware to reach new markets both at home and abroad. So convenient for transport was the new canal, that Wedgwood's stayed at Etruria until 1940, but by then subsidence and polution threatened their canalside premises and they moved out into the countryside at Barlaston. The new works had six electric tunnel ovens replacing the bottle-shaped kilns which had become so synonymous with the Potteries.

Part of the new plant includes a Visitor Centre, where the general public can watch and talk with skilled craftsmen at work in the various stages of production.

Also included in the price of admission is the chance to see a film on the history of Wedgwood or the techniques of pottery production. There is also a fine museum exhibiting famous Wedgwood designs from down the years, including examples of the world famous blue & white Jasper ware and an intriguing collection of samples used by Josiah Wedgwood in the perfection of Jasper. After you've been around the centre you can have some refreshment and perhaps buy a souvenir of your visit at the factory shop.

INFORMATION

Location: 2 minutes walk from Bridge 104.
Open times: Mon-Fri, 9-17.00 all year round.
Admission: Adults 50p, children 25p.
Children under 5 not admitted.
Tel: Barlaston (078139) 4141.

20 TRENT & MERSEY CANAL 23mls/13hrs Middlewich — Great Haywood 9mls/4hrs

THE CANAL FOLLOWS the valley of the river Trent, passing through the Meaford flight in open country — locals pronounce it 'Method' and not 'Meeford'! On summer weekends this is a popular spot. Cars line the verge and 'gongoozlers' (canal folks' term for members of the public who lean on bridge parapets or loll by locksides with vacant expressions) watch your progress through the locks. You begin to feel quite important given this 'star' treatment. But then it goes to your head and you try to push the balance beam the wrong way or drop your windlass in the water!

The triangular pool which issues from the short pound below the top Meaford lock shows where the canal descended through a three-chambered staircase lock prior to 1830. A staircase lock is one where chambers are telescoped together — the top gates of one chamber forming the bottom gates of the next. Examples are still in use at other points on the inland waterways — notably at Bingley on the Leeds & Liverpool Canal where there are five connected chambers — but you won't encounter any on the FOUR COUNTIES RING.

Above Meaford Locks the canal — bordered by yellow-red Monkey-flower, mauve Willow Herb and boggy bushes that hide it from the railway — prowls the rusty perimeter fence of a power station; the first, geographically, of many which use the cool waters of the Trent all along its course to the Humber, indigenous to the Trent as castles to the Rhine. This one always seems strangely withdrawn and introspective; people-less, railway sidings empty of wagons, cooling towers bereft of steam, a *Marie Celeste* among power stations.

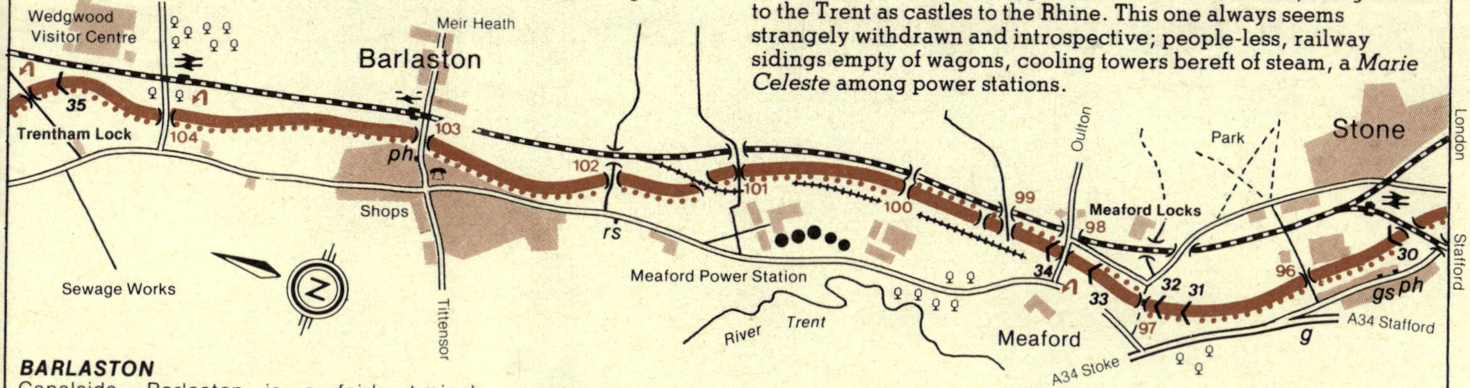

BARLASTON

Canalside, Barlaston is a fairly typical residential suburb. Pleasant enough for its inhabitants but with little to catch the eye for the visitor. Over the level crossing and up the wooded hill to the East, however, matters improve, the road opening out by a pretty green. The old, dilapidated Palladian style hall has recently been secured by conservationists from Wedgwoods, and there are hopes that it may be restored.

EATING & DRINKING

PLUME OF FEATHERS — Bass. Canalside Bridge 103.
LAKESIDE GOLF & COUNTRY CLUB — 100 yards from Bridge 102. Bar lunches, restaurant meals in the evenings and Sunday lunch. Squash £2.70 per session inc. racquet hire. A round of golf from £4. Trout fishing if you've brought your own rod!

SHOPPING

Grocer, butcher, newsagent, chemist & Co-op 3 mins from Bridge 103.

PLACES TO VISIT

WEDGWOOD VISITOR CENTRE — see opposite.

PUBLIC TRANSPORT

BUSES — Potteries Motor Traction service 45, hourly Mon-Sat to/from Stoke & Hanley.
TRAINS — Local trains to/from Stoke, Stafford & Birmingham, approx bi-hourly Mon-Sat.

21 TRENT & MERSEY CANAL 27mls/15hrs Middlewich — Great Haywood 6mls/2½hrs

EVEN THESE DAYS STONE, once headquarters of the Trent & Mersey Canal Company, is a flourishing canal centre with three hire fleets, a chandlery, and plenty of interesting moored boats to talk about as you chug through the locks. Between Locks 28 and 29 you pass part of the sadly closed Joule's brewery, whose Stone Ale was famous in North Staffordshire. Rationalisation saw the brewery submerged by the Bass Charrington conglomerate in 1970, and brewing ceased 4 years later. Joules had been brewing in Stone since 1758 and with the coming of the canal they were able to expand their markets, exporting to America and Europe via the Trent & Mersey connected ports of Liverpool and Hull. As late as the 1950s Joule's Stone offices retained the telephone number 'Stone 1'! South of Stone the canal meanders across a quiet pastoral landscape. Cattle come down to the water to drink, moorhens construct precarious nests, rabbits look furtively up from 'silflay' and herons patrol their beats. For the boat steerer it's a time for peaceful reflection; what a holiday on the canals is really all about.

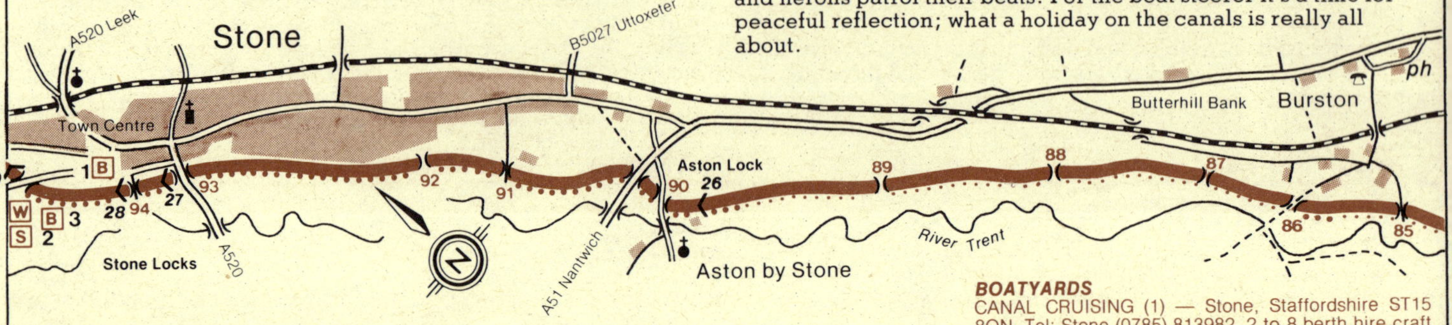

STONE
High Street is a bustling thoroughfare with its fair share of valuable buildings, perhaps the best of which is the 18th century Crown Hotel. Plaques on walls at intervals tell us that the landscape watercolourist Peter de Wint was born here, that the Duke of Cumberland came here to fight, and that the Star Inn has long attended to the thirst of waterborne by-passers. We liked Stone a lot!

EATING & DRINKING
STAR INN — Bass, sandwiches & pies. Canalside lock 27. *Poky little place with good atmosphere.*
RISING SUN — Bass & snacks. By Lock 30, Map 20.
CROWN HOTEL — High Street.
Plenty of other good pubs in town centre.

SHOPPING
EC Wed, MD Tue & Thur
All facilities, a good centre for shopping, moor below Lock 27 for best access. Sunday morning gs above top Lock No.30, newsagent opposite PO North end of High Street. Good bookshop (new & secondhand) by Bridge 94.

PUBLIC TRANSPORT
BUSES — Potteries Motor Traction to/from Stoke & Stafford. Radical timetable changes as we went to press. Tel: Stoke (0782) 48811.
TRAINS — ¼m E of top lock (Map 20). Local trains to/from Stafford, Stoke & Birmingham, bi-hourly Mon-Sat. Tel: Stoke (0782) 411411. *Nice Jacobean station house.*

BOATYARDS
CANAL CRUISING (1) — Stone, Staffordshire ST15 8QN. Tel: Stone (0785) 813982. 2 to 8 berth hire craft (Blakes). Pumpout, diesel, Calor gas, rubbish disposal, short-term moorings, repairs & servicing, drydock, crane, boatbuilding, sales & brokerage.
MIDLAND LUXURY CRUISERS (2) — Newcastle Road, Stone, Staffs. Tel: Stone 816871. 2 to 12 berth hire craft (Hoseasons). Pumpout, Elsan disposal, diesel, water, rubbish disposal, Calor gas, repairs & servicing, slipway, moorings, boat sales & brokerage.
STONE BOATBUILDING (3) — Newcastle Road, Stone, Staffs. Tel: Stone 812688. Chandlery & canalia, slipway & moorings.

BURSTON
Little hamlet whose houses look out onto a reedy duck pond.

EATING & DRINKING
THE GREYHOUND INN — Burtonwood & food. *Good country pub.*

22 TRENT & MERSEY CANAL 31mls/17hrs Middlewich — Great Haywood 3mls/1hr

A DELIGHTFUL LENGTH of waterway with locks at the most satisfying intervals. The Trent Valley is at its lovliest. Wooded Hopton Heath, scene of a Civil War skirmish in 1643, lies above the village of Salt to the South-west, whilst the landscaped parkland of Sandon Hall with its slender urn-topped column commemorating Prime Minister William Pitt encompasses views to the North-east.
Railway, road and canal share the same narrow defile — how often this is the case — modes of transport change but not their routes. The trains — London Euston to Manchester — are pulled by electric locomotives, many of which are named. Our research crew 'spotted' *Vesta, Sir Laurence Olivier, Knight of the Thistle* and *William Webb Ellis;* stirring stuff!
Weston Hall sits aloofly high up out of the village on the Stafford road. It is a wise old Jacobean mansion, mullioned, solid and dependable. Its windows would have watched Brindley's wild navies digging their way through the then, and relatively still, unspoilt river valley.

NB. Boats should keep to the centre channel for the canal is deceptively shallow.

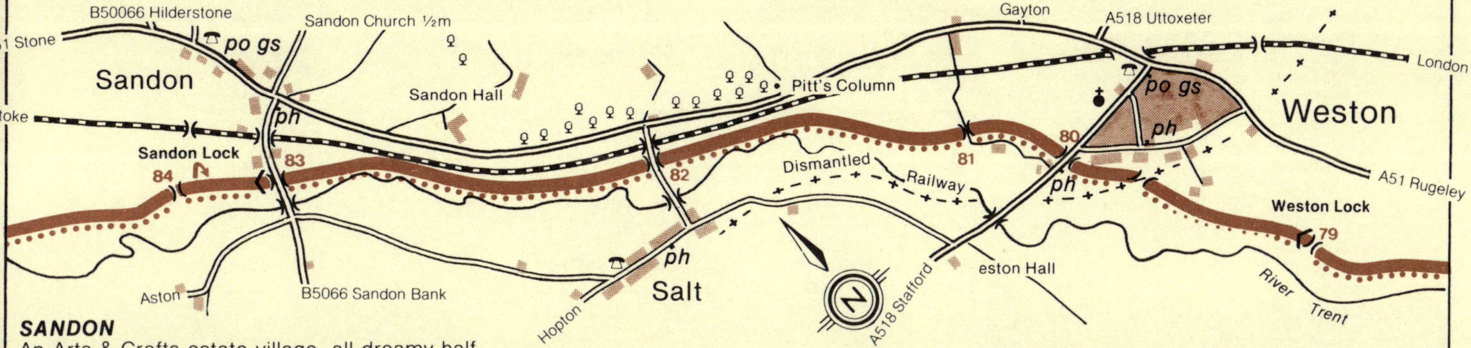

SANDON

An Arts & Crafts estate village, all dreamy half timber. The war memorial — a sentinel infantryman — reminds us that only politicians win wars. You can walk up the hill with the pheasants to the church of All Saints, and from the churchyard see the Trent Valley spreading out below you.

EATING & DRINKING

DOG & DOUBLET — Bass, bar food, evening meals & accommodation. *Time has passed this lovely pub by, it even has the old fashioned decency to stay shut on Sundays!*

SHOPPING

Post office stores open weekdays except Sat pm.

SALT

From the ornate Norman like arch of Bridge 82 it's only 5 minutes walk across the river to this one-time salt producing village.

EATING & DRINKING

THE HOLLYBUSH — Burtonwood, bar grills & garden. *Pretty little pub reputedly one of the oldest in England.*

WESTON

You can sit by the village green outside The Woolpack after a hard day's canaling. Two famous Victorian architects — Gilbert Scott and William Butterfield — have left their mark on the Perpendicular spired church.

EATING & DRINKING

THE WOOLPACK — M&B, bar lunches Mon-Sat, dinner Fri & Sat; table skittles.
SARACEN'S HEAD — Bass, lunches, garden, canalside by Bridge 80.

SHOPPING

Post office stores open daily including Sun am.

PUBLIC TRANSPORT

BUSES — From PO: Stevensons 404, 6 each way Mon-Sat, to/from Stafford & Uttoxeter. Tel: Burton (0283) 63318.

Nature Book

Yellow Iris

IT SEEMS odd that of all the beautiful flowers growing wild in the British countryside such a large number of the very best should be found thriving in or near water. Some are brightly coloured and others prolific or possessed of enormous blooms while a few combine all these qualities in ostentious displays of florid extravagance. To my mind the Yellow Iris, or Flag, is just such a plant. From May through to the end of July great clumps of aureate blooms betray the tropical origins of a flower far too exotic to have evolved in these temperate climes.

GROWING to three or more feet in height the iris can be readily identified even when not in flower by the tall sword-like leaves. Spreading out alternately from the base of the plant and varying in colour from khaki through to bright emerald the leaves are as obvious on the canal bank as the flowers themselves. From the middle of a dense spray of leaves arise several multi-branched stems each leaved and bearing as many as four bright yellow flowers. The topmost flower opens first while the remaining buds stay tightly furled until the flower directly above each has bloomed, been fertilised and faded away. From our point of view this is all very nice because it means that the flowering of a particular plant will be extended over the longest possible period, while the plant benefits from each individual flower having the greatest opportunity of being cross-pollinated.

THE IRIS family rely entirely upon insects for pollination. When a bee, or any other insect, arrives at a flower seeking nectar it alights at the base of one of the three large petaloid perianths and thrusts its head deep into the body of the flower. In doing so it brushes first against the female parts of the flower and there deposits any pollen it may have picked up from another flower and then, as it pushes further into the flower, against the male anthers and thus collects more pollen. By this arrangement the iris minimises the risk of self pollination.

THE SEEDS develop inside a small marrow-shaped capsule about 2 inches long which eventually dries out and splits into three segments, scattering the seeds. The mature plant overwinters in the mud as a rhizome which can be transplanted in late autumn, though I warn anyone considering introducing a Yellow Iris into their garden that once you've got one . . .!

Marcus Potts

23 STAFFS & WORCS CANAL 35mls/18½hrs Middlewich — Autherley Jnct 19mls/9hrs

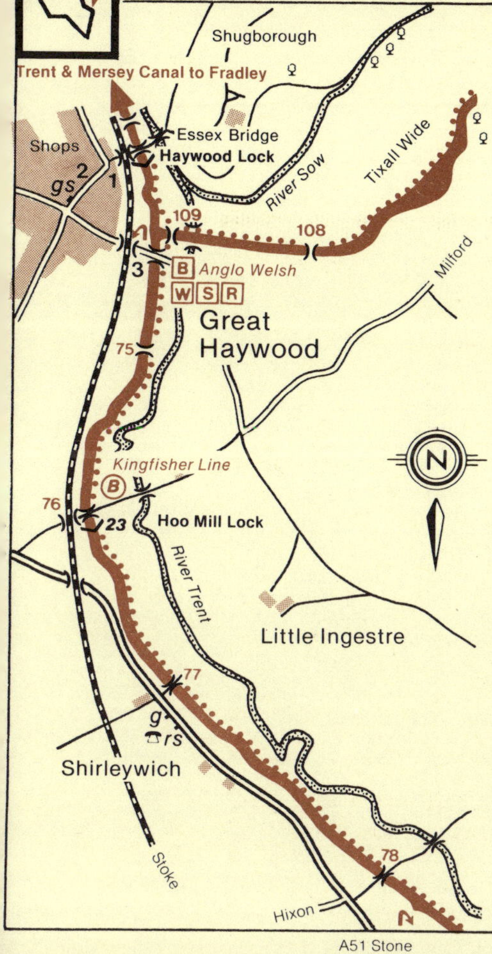

AT THE CONFLUENCE of the rivers Sow and Trent, Brindley brought his Staffordshire & Worcestershire Canal along the former's valley to meet with his Trent & Mersey Canal. Great Haywood thus became a canal junction of major importance, as significant to transport in the 18th century as any motorway interchange today. With the completion of the S&W in 1772 and the T&M five years later, Great Haywood saw goods passing through to and from the four great English estuaries of Humber, Thames, Severn and Mersey; James Brindley's dream of a 'Grand Cross' had been fulfilled.

Two of the most beautiful bridges in the whole of England are to be found at Great Haywood! One you will cruise under if you are doing the FOUR COUNTIES RING. Numbered Bridge 109 on the Staffs & Worcs Canal, it carrys the Trent & Mersey towpath across the 'mouth' of the S&W upon the slenderest of brick arches; an 18th century miracle of functional engineering and enduring beauty. The other bridge is tucked away at the village's bosky behind, hidden from all but the most inquisitive canal travellers. But if you are to visit Shugborough (see below) on foot you must perforce cross its cutwatered span. It is a packhorse bridge of old England, built at the behest of the 1st Earl of Essex in the 16th century to ease the passage of his hunting parties on their way to Cannock Chase.

A mile West of the junction, the Staffs & Worcs, having crossed the river Trent on a low slung aqueduct, suddenly widens into a reedy lake inhabited by grebe, mallard, moorhen and kingfisher. This is Tixall wide and there are two theories for its existence. Some say that the canal was widened into an artificial lake to placate the owner of Tixall Hall, others that the pool predates the canal and that Izaak Walton learnt his trade here.

GREAT HAYWOOD

EATING & DRINKING

CLIFFORD ARMS (1) — Bass & snacks.
COACH & HORSES — Restaurant & motel, bar snacks. Canalside by Bridge 77.

SHOPPING

Post office (1), Spar min-mart & newsagency (open Sun am), butcher, hardware store (Calor gas) and local crafts shop (2). Canalside farm-shop & cafe (3) for fresh fruit and vegetables.

PLACES TO VISIT

SHUGBOROUGH — pedestrian access W of Essex Bridge, 5 mins walk from junction. Mansion & gardens open Mar-Oct, Tue-Fri 10-5.30, Sat & Sun 2-5.30: County Museum as Mansion plus Oct-Mar, Tue-Fri 10.30-4.30 & 1st & 3rd Sundays 2-4.30. Farm, Mar-Oct, Sat & Sun only 2-6. Admission 60p adults, 30p children, each to mansion & museum (ie total £1.20); farm 25p adults, 15p children. 17/18th century house home of the Anson family. Staffordshire's excellent County Museum located in former stable block. Farm has rare breeds and old farming implements. Tel: Little Haywood (0889) 881388.

BOATYARDS

ANGLO WELSH — HQ, 3 The Basin, Market Harborough, LE16 7BJ. Tel: MH (0858) 66910. 2 to 10 berth hire craft. Pumpout, Elsan disposal, water, diesel, Shell gas, rubbish disposal, repairs & servicing, crane, small canalia & chandlery selection. Boatyard telephone Little Haywood 881711.

KINGFISHER LINE — Hoo Mill Lock, Great Haywood, Staffs ST18 0RG. Tel: Little Haywood (0889) 881384. Day boats for hire. Pumpout, diesel, Calor gas, moorings, repairs & servicing, drydock, boatbuilding, sales & brokerage, chandlery, canalia, groceries & coffees.

24 STAFFS & WORCS CANAL 2mls/½hr Great Haywood — Autherley Jnct 16mls/7hrs

BRACKENY CANNOCK CHASE and wooded Shugborough form an exquisite horizon to the South. Those with infinite leisure can moor by Bridge 106 and explore the footpaths which criss-cross the deer-inhabited Chase from Milford Green.

This is the length of canal so evocatively described in "Narrow Boat", where L.T.C. Rolt, cruising aboard *Cressy* in the Autumn of 1939, met the elderly lock-keeper at Tixall and is told that *Cressy* is the first boat to pass by in 6 months!

The canal crosses the river Sow by way of a typical Brindley designed acqueduct, carrying the whole weight of puddled clay canal bed within its sturdy frame. The pillbox is, of course, a later addition from the last war when canals were considered important lines of defence in the event of invasion.

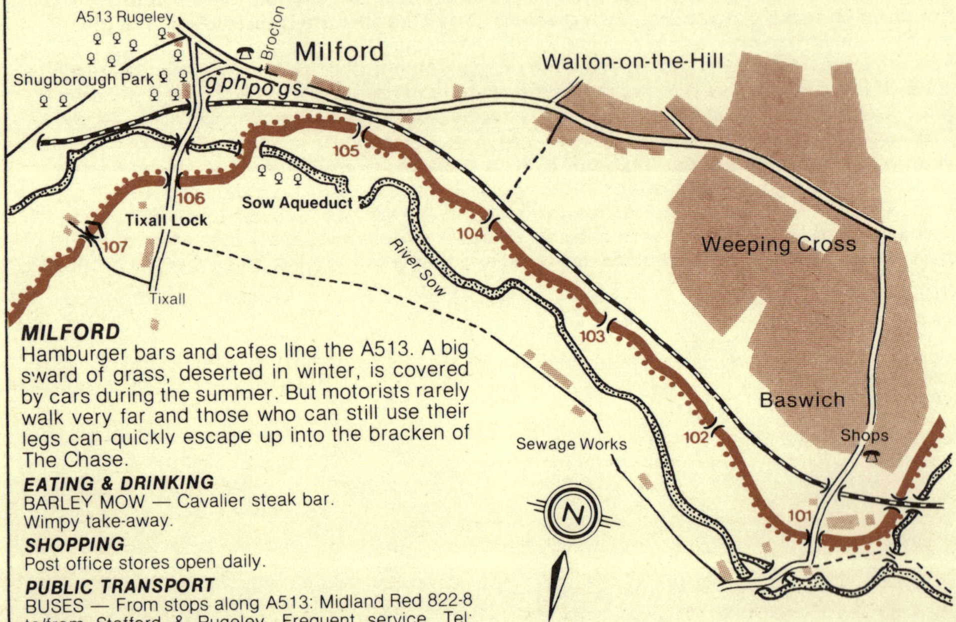

MILFORD

Hamburger bars and cafes line the A513. A big sward of grass, deserted in winter, is covered by cars during the summer. But motorists rarely walk very far and those who can still use their legs can quickly escape up into the bracken of The Chase.

EATING & DRINKING

BARLEY MOW — Cavalier steak bar.
Wimpy take-away.

SHOPPING

Post office stores open daily.

PUBLIC TRANSPORT

BUSES — From stops along A513: Midland Red 822-8 to/from Stafford & Rugeley. Frequent service. Tel: Stafford (0785) 42997.

STAFFORD

Frustratingly just too far away from the canal for the average holidaymaker to visit, but those with more time at their disposal may enjoy exploring this under-rated county town. The parish church of St Mary's with its fine central tower dates from the 13th century, though much restored by Gilbert Scott in the 1840's. Nearby, Church Lane, is a pretty cobbled thoroughfare. Numerous Victorian county offices lend an almost metropolitan air to the proceedings. Ironically, the river Sow used to be navigable to old wharves which stood in the centre of Stafford, and the old towing path provides possibly the most appropriate route into the town from Bridge 101 (25-30 mins walk). Alternatively, catch a bus from opposite the Trumpet Grill by Bridge 98 (Map 25).

EATING & DRINKING

THE SOUP KITCHEN — Church Lane, town centre. Mon-Sat, EC Wed. *Quaint & bustling coffee house.*

SHOPPING

EC Wed, MD Tue, Fri & Sat.
All services. First class shopping centre. Useful suburban shops 5 mins S of Bridge 101.

PLACES TO VISIT

STAFFORD MUSEUM & ART GALLERY — The Green, Stafford. Open Tue-Sat, admission free. Sad little museum which seems to have been left behind by the prestigious developments at Shugborough.
WILLIAM SALT LIBRARY — Eastgate Street, Stafford. Open Tue-Sat, admission free. Staffordshire history; really for the specialist.
TOURIST INFORMATION CENTRE — Civic Offices, Riverside, Stafford. Tel: Stafford (0782) 3181. Useful leaflets & town trail.

continued overleaf

Tixall Lock

Nature Book

The Moorhen

THE CHANCES are that the first animal spotted by the waterway traveller today is the Moorhen, *Gallinula chloropus*. More common on the still waters of the canals than its larger relative, the Coot, the Moorhen is one of the world's most widespread birds. Present on every continent except the Poles, its success is largely due to a ready ability to adapt to man-made environments. "Moorhen" has nothing to do with moors but is a derivation of Merehen, bird of the lakes, and practically any patch of weed-bordered water is a suitable habitat for this most versatile of birds.

JERKING its head back and forth as it swims or flicking its white tail flash the adult Moorhen, black all over save for the white patches on flank and tail, is easy enough to identify. The red forehead also distinguishes it from the bald-headed Coot, though the two are rarely seen together. It is a prolific breeder and can lay batches of from 5 to 11 eggs any time between April and September, a mature bird often achieving as many as three broods in a single season. The nest is normally a tangle of reeds or flags bent over at the base and still alive but this agile bird will sometimes venture further afield and the higher branches of an overhanging tree are not considered too much of a challenge. The young, looking like balls of black cotton wool, hatch after three weeks and are out and about only two or three days later. As they grow they lose the black fluff and develop into drab grey versions of their parents.

THOUGH able to fly after only about six weeks the Moorhen prefers to escape from its predators on foot; scurrying rapidly over land and water with a mad flurry of wings and metallic trim-phone noises. But the Moorhen is a shy bird rarely taken unawares and an individual seen in the distance is likely to have disappeared almost without trace by the time the boat reaches the spot. This habit makes adult Moorhens poor parents as they leave helpless chicks to fend for themselves in the open waters of the canal. Of a large brood possibly only two or three will survive the first few weeks while fewer still reach maturity. A fact to which the adult Moorhen will merely "clock-clock" in disapproval and strut off to prepare for the next generation.

Marcus Potts

DEPTMORE LOCK IS OUT in the wilds. Statuesque conifers stand about the lock-side like the ghosts of old boatmen. The man in the rose-clad, whitewashed cottage commutes by dinghy for no road ever got this far. It's heron country too; see them ponderously flap away across the damp watermeadows of the Penk, a tributary of the Sow that the canal follows as far as the market town of Penkridge.

NB. Take care cruising through Bridge 98. Use the white markers to line your boat up, and keep off the cabin roof.

A relentless drone fills the landscape. It emanates from the M6 motorway. There are those who feel that each successive mode of transport invented is less civilised than its predecessor. It's not so much the motorways themselves, time will bed them into the landscape as tidily as it has had to accommodate the canals and railways before, but their cacaphonous procession of motor car and lorry. Yet perhaps the time will come when transport needs change to leave the motorways gathering moss and weeds, and then some entrepeneur will have the great idea of selling nostalgic motorway holidays!

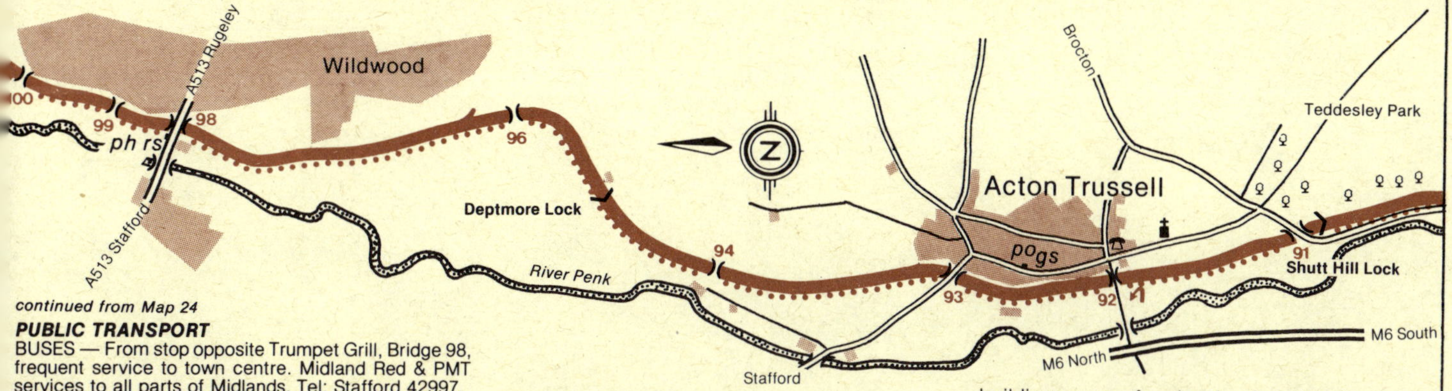

continued from Map 24

PUBLIC TRANSPORT

BUSES — From stop opposite Trumpet Grill, Bridge 98, frequent service to town centre. Midland Red & PMT services to all parts of Midlands. Tel: Stafford 42997.
TRAINS — Town centre, 1½m W of canal. Major railhead. Tel: Stoke (0785) 411411.

STAFFORD

See Map 24

EATING & DRINKING

THE TRUMPET INN — Toby steak bar plus bar food Mon-Fri. Canalside by Bridge 98.

ACTON TRUSSELL

The name conjures visions of a picture-book English village, but what village there was has been suffocated by modern dormitory housing; a typical village of the Motor Age. The old church sensibly shuns 20th century reality clinging to its peaceful hilltop. Even the farm buildings are facelessly functional. Sorry *Actonites*, but we expected so much and you let us down so badly!

EATING & DRINKING

None!

SHOPPING

Post Office stores & newsagency, open daily inc Sun am.

26 STAFFS & WORCS CANAL   9mls/4hrs Great Haywood — Autherley Jnct 8mls/3hrs

LOCKS COME THICK AND FAST as the Staffs & Worcs ascends to and descends from its summit level. The M6 retreats only to be replaced by the gable to gable 3-ups, 2-downs which cling-wrap Penkridge. Yet a mile either side of the canal the countryside is a lonely unvisited region of rolling farmland lifting eastwards to Cannock Chase.

Historically, this is an interesting section of canal. South of the railway bridge adjoining Bridge 81, where Willow Herb hugs the motorway embankment, there used to be a thriving transhipment wharf. Here, coal brought from the Chase-side collieries by mineral line was loaded onto dayboats to be taken to the factory furnaces of the Black Country. The wharf was abandoned in 1949, the last regular traffic being in the boats of T.S. Element to Stourport power station.

Bridge 89 is a balustraded affair, nicknamed "Fancy Bridge" by the old boatmen. It was built to carry the carriageway to Teddesley Hall, a mansion demolished in the 1950s after being used as a POW camp during the Second World War.

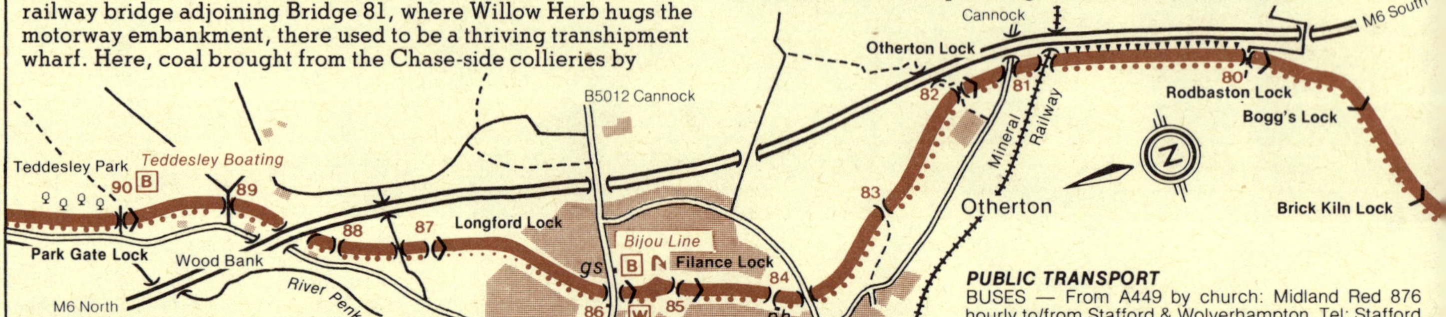

PENKRIDGE

The wharfside is pretty, the towpath tunnelling beneath the Cannock road. Five minutes walk takes you to the narrow main street, a pleasant place to shop and saunter. The impressive red sandstone church was one of the county's six collegiate churches, second only in importance to a cathedral and with its own Dean. Half a mile beyond the railway the picturesque Cuttlestone Bridge spans the river Penk.

EATING & DRINKING

THE BOAT — Ind Coope, canalside by Bridge 86.
THE STAR (1) — Bank's & lunches Mon-Sat.
THE CROSS KEYS — Bass (Springfield & Brew XI), meals Mon-Sat lunch & evening, canalside patio. Canalside by Bridge 84. *Popular with boaters, lots of canal decorations, but much changed from the unvisited canal inn described in Rolt's "Narrow Boat".*

COFFEE CORNER (2) — open Mon-Sat 9-5 (ex Tue) & Sun lunch. *Pleasing "Just A Bite" recommended eatery.*

SHOPPING

EC Wed, MD Wed & Sat.
All services. Good shopping. The thriving market is held in the fields beside the river (3). Summerhouse Stores by Bridge 86 is open daily inc Sun am.

PUBLIC TRANSPORT

BUSES — From A449 by church: Midland Red 876 hourly to/from Stafford & Wolverhampton. Tel: Stafford (0785) 42997. Warstone's 471 to/from Cannock. Tel: Cheslyn Hay (0922) 414141.
TRAINS — station ½m W of canal, local trains to/from Birmingham, Wolverhampton & Stafford. Tel: Stoke (0782) 411411. No Sunday service.

BOATYARDS

TEDDESLEY BOAT COMPANY — Teddesley Road, Penkridge, Staffs ST19 5RH. Tel: Penkridge (078571) 4692. 4 to 8 berth hire craft (Hoseasons). Pumpout, Elsan disposal, water, diesel, Calor gas, rubbish disposal, payphone, moorings, repairs & servicing, slipway, crane, boatbuilding, specialists in grit blasting of boat hulls.
MIDLAND CHANDLERS — as above. Tel: Penkridge 2437. Comprehensive chandlery, boat fittings & accessories.
BIJOU LINE — 27 Penkridge Wharf, Penkridge, Staffs. Tel: Penkridge 2732. 2 to 10 berth hire craft. Pumpout, Calor gas, repairs & servicing, canalia.

27 STAFFS & WORCS CANAL 13mls/6hrs Great Haywood — Autherley Jnct 4mls/1½hrs

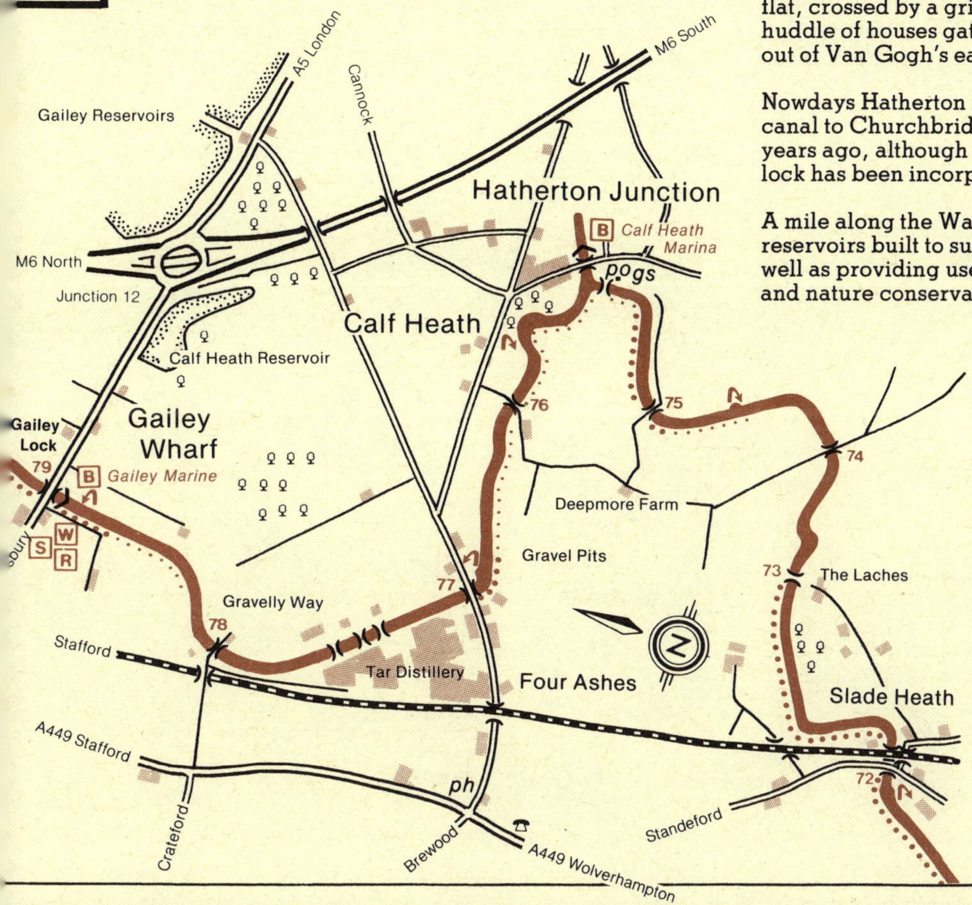

CALF HEATH is an isolated, melancholy landscape, pancake flat, crossed by a grid of sullen roads, with here and there a huddle of houses gathered reassuringly together like something out of Van Gogh's early potato field paintings.

Nowdays Hatherton is a junction only in name, for the former canal to Churchbridge and Cannock closed to navigation twenty years ago, although it is still used as a water feeder and the first lock has been incorporated in the adjacent boatyard.

A mile along the Watling Street from Gailey Wharf are three reservoirs built to supply the canal with water. They still do, as well as providing useful amenities such as dinghy sailing, fishing and nature conservation.

GAILEY WHARF

A circular, turreted former toll-keeper's house dominates the scene and would, in days gone by, have offered the toll clerk good views of boats climbing up from Penkridge to the summit level.

BOATYARDS

GAILEY MARINE — The Wharf, Watling Street, Gailey, Stafford. Tel: Standeford (0902) 790612. 4 to 8 berth hire craft (Blue Riband Club). Pumpout, Elsan disposal, Calor gas, repairs & servicing, boatbuilding, canalia.

HATHERTON JUNCTION

Little more than a former canal junction and a row of villas. A new mooring lagoon is being dug out. Nearby the canal pierces the pungent heart of a tar distillery.

EATING & DRINKING

Cafe at boatyard Mon, Wed, Fri-Sun.

SHOPPING

Post office stores at boatyard.

BOATYARDS

CALF HEATH MARINA — Calf Heath, Cannock, Staffs. Tel: Standeford (0902) 790909. 2 to 8 berth hire craft (Boat Enquiries). Pumpout, water, Calor gas, moorings, repairs & servicing, drydock, slipway, crane, canalia.

28 STAFFS & WORCS CANAL 17mls/8hrs Great Haywood

FOR A COUPLE OF MILES, with Autherley Junction almost in the centre, the route of the FOUR COUNTIES RING passes through the fourth county which justifies its name — West Midlands; one of the new counties which sprang up after the local government changes of 1974. Uncannily the canal becomes as dull as the county name! But happily this is only a brief interlude, things rapidly improve, whether you're heading up the Shropshire Union (see Map 1) or the Staffs & Worcs which breaks out into open country at Coven Heath.

NB 1. Boaters cruising The Ring in a clockwise direction should turn right at Autherley Junction under Bridge 1 and into the Stop Lock, turning to Map 1 to follow their route up the Shropshire Union Canal.

NB 2. Between Bridges 67 & 68 the Staffs & Worcs Canal narrows and there is no room for boats to pass each other: proceed with caution.

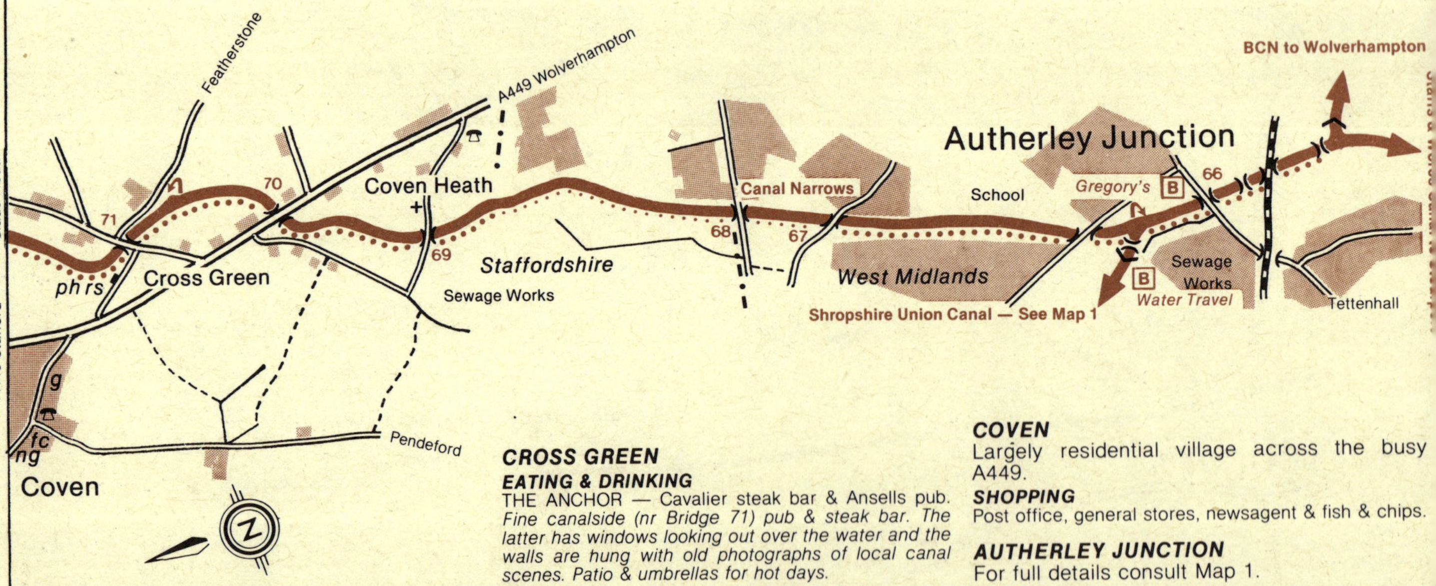

CROSS GREEN

EATING & DRINKING

THE ANCHOR — Cavalier steak bar & Ansells pub. *Fine canalside (nr Bridge 71) pub & steak bar. The latter has windows looking out over the water and the walls are hung with old photographs of local canal scenes. Patio & umbrellas for hot days.*

COVEN

Largely residential village across the busy A449.

SHOPPING

Post office, general stores, newsagent & fish & chips.

AUTHERLEY JUNCTION

For full details consult Map 1.

Better Boating

Helpful hints for those new (and not so new) to canal cruising.

LOCKING

Working a lock is like your first kiss — until you've done it no amount of reading about it beforehand can quite prepare you for the experience! Most reputable boat hire firms will ensure that first-timers are given a demonstration in lock usage and, if there are locks near the base, will actually take you through one under their tutelage. However, once you're out on your own, having grasped the basic principals, here are one or two suggestions to help add a bit more finesse to your efforts.

● Plan ahead using the maps, and as you near a lock let the member(s) of your crew who is(are) going to operate the lock ashore; the nearest bridgehole is usually a good spot.

● When the lock operator arrives at a lock which is found to be against them — ie it has to be filled or emptied before your boat can use it — they should first check that no other boat is approaching from the opposite direction which could use the lock first; thus saving some 20,000 gallons of precious water.

● Now operate the lock, sharing the chamber if there is room for you and another boat close behind (the combined length should not exceed 70ft). If a steel boat is sharing a lock with a fibre-glass boat then the steel boat should always go in first.

● Go about your lock drill slowly and methodically. Open paddles slowly, especially going uphill, and if there are gate paddles open them after the ground paddles. Never run near the chamber edge. If there are onlookers, particularly children, don't let them get in your way. (A note here about children and locks — yes, they can help and moreover enjoy contributing. But if they are your children only trust them to do what you know they are capable of, and if they're not yours then we advise you to think twice before letting them take part).

● Never leave windlasses on the paddle spindles; if the paddle slipped they could spin off and cause serious injury.

● Leave gate paddles up until you've used the gates, as this will help reduce water resistance and make opening and closing easier.

● When you leave a lock always make sure that you've wound down all the paddles. One left up could result in the canal running dry. Always close all the gates as well, the only exception to this rule being if there is a boat approaching which could conveniently use the lock, at such times it is polite to leave the gates open for them.

● Check that you have your windlass with you when you leave a lock.

● When passing through a lock the boat steerer should ensure that the boat is kept under control, keeping it clear of the cill (ledge) at the top of the chamber when going downhill, and clear of any protruding metalwork on the bottom gates when going uphill. It is not necessary to use ropes to steady steel boats in locks.

● Finally, as you quickly get the hang of lock working, it becomes a most pleasurable activity; you even begin to look forward to the next lock, the chance to stretch your legs and perhaps chat with other boaters. But never relax your vigilance. Concentrate on the job and you won't go far wrong.

RUNNING AGROUND

On most parts of the FOUR COUNTIES RING the canal will be no deeper than 3 or 4 feet. Keep to the channel and grounding will be a rare occurence, but here's what to do if you do hit the mud!

● As you feel the boat running up onto the mud ease off the throttle and stop the boat by using reverse. This will normally cause the stern (back) to move out into deeper water. If it does, all well and good, reverse out the way you come, regain the channel and resume your journey. If you're still stuck, then bring everyone on board away from where the boat is grounded and place them where the boat is in deeper water and repeat the reversing operation. If you're still well and truly stuck then use the poles/shafts provided to push the stern out into deeper water. Don't push at the bows (front) this will only pivot you further onto the mud.

● One of the most frequent reasons for going aground is trying to give oncoming boats too much room when passing. Ease off when passing, aim to give the approaching boat 2 or 3 feet of space between you and all should be well.

TURNING

Short boats of under 25ft should be able to turn at any point in the canal. Longer than that and you'll need a junction, boatyard basin or winding hole. The latter (pronounced as the thing which blows and not as you would expect the thing that turns!) are provided at intervals for lengthy craft to turn in — they are marked . . . thus on the maps. Always drive in the bows (front) first so that your stern remains in deepest water. Then with a judicious mixture of forward and reverse let the boat turn itself round.

STEERING

Other than the obvious advice about tiller steering — push the tiller to the left to turn to the right and push to the right to turn to the left — there are one or two other hints which could be useful.

- The boat pivots on a point about a third of the way back from the bows (front); keep an eye on this point and aim to keep it in the deepest part of the canal.
- When faced with strong cross-winds it may be necessary to steer the boat slightly sideways along the canal. When doing this try to keep the stern in the deepest water and remember to allow for the wind when approaching bridges or locks.
- At some points on the FOUR COUNTIES RING bypass weirs around locks may gush out across the foot of the lock. Be prepared for the bows to be effected by the flow and compensate by steering into the flow. Also keep the boat away from the weirs at the top of the locks.
- Very few boats with tiller steering can be controlled in reverse. The only way to maintain direction in reverse is to interrupt with short bursts of forward to retain the desired line.

MOORING

You may moor almost anywhere along the canal on the towpath side. You may not moor: on the non-towpath side (except at legitimate boatyard moorings); on tight bends; opposite turning points or junctions; next to facilities except when using them; within 100ft of a bridge or lock; between locks in flights of locks.

- Slow down as your approach your chosen mooring. Take the bows (front) of the boat in first and put the engine in neutral. Put someone ashore and let them pull your stern (rear) in.

- Never pass your mooring ropes over the towpath if you can help it. However, if the towpath is so narrow that you have to in order to make a secure mooring, then give adequate indication that your ropes are crossing the path — ie tie a white cloth around the rope so that anyone using the path can see the obstacle.
- Insert mooring stakes at an angle to the ground sloping away from the boat with either both in from the ends of the boat or both out.
- Return the rope to the boat after securing it to the mooring pin. This will give you a 2 to 1 pulley ratio and will help in drawing the boat closer to the bank.

Choosing a good mooring spot for the night is especially important. Whether you want to be gregarious and close to the nearest pub, or well out in the peace and quiet of the countryside is up to you. Follow the above advice and you won't go far wrong. Note that some boatyards charge for overnight mooring within their boundary.

TUNNELS

Tunnels are fun! Passing through a canal tunnel can be the highlight of your holiday, but the following points may be useful.

- Tunnels tend to drip, so wear waterproofs and a hood or hat.
- Switch on your headlight as you approach the tunnel and don't forget to switch it off as you emerge at the other end.
- Children usually love the experience of passing through a tunnel, but it is only the steerer standing in the dark at the back of the boat who appreciates the possible dangers. If someone did fall overboard in the darkness they might not be missed until arrival at the far end. So keep young children (and pet animals too) in sight, and preferably, inside the boat.
- Don't ever stay on the roof of a boat in a tunnel.

SPEED

- A speed limit of 4mph exists throughout the FOUR COUNTIES RING. However, as boats are not equipped with speedometers this rule tends to be widely interpreted. Moreover, a boat travelling at 4mph along a shallow length of canal can create quite sizeable waves which wash away the canal banks. In effect there is only one firm, not to be broken rule governing your speed, and that is that you should not be making a wash or wave.
- You should always slow right down when passing moored boats or fishermen.

Information

Passenger Trip Boats

If you haven't the time or inclination to take a full canal holiday, then a good alternative and an excellent way of sampling the canal is to take a trip aboard one of the passenger boats which run public and charter outings along sections of the FOUR COUNTIES RING. Further details from:
Steam Cruising Co. Ltd. Tel: Woodseaves (078 574) 529. *Horse-drawn (despite the name) trips along the Shropshire Union Canal between Norbury and Market Drayton.*
Potteries Canal Cruising Co. Tel: Stoke (0782) 657507. *Cruises along the Trent & Mersey Canal from Hem Heath, Trentham.*
M.E. Braine. Brownhills (054 33) 4888. *Trips from Great Haywood.*

Navigable Dimensions

Maximum length—72ft
Maximum width—6ft 10in
Maximum draught—3ft
Maximum headroom—5ft 9in

Harecastle Tunnel

A timetable operates through the 'single-lane' Harecastle Tunnel. From 1st April to 31st October craft travelling in either direction on weekdays Monday to Friday may enter the tunnel as instructed by the tunnel keeper at either end between 8 am and 4 pm. On Sat, Sun and Bank Holidays, Northbound craft may enter the tunnel between dawn and 1 pm, Southbound craft between 3 pm and dusk and also on Friday evenings between 7 pm and dusk. From 1st November to 31st March Northbound craft may enter the tunnel between dawn and 11.30 am, Southbound craft between 1.30 pm and dusk. Canoes, unpowered craft and pedestrians are prohibited from using the tunnel.

Useful Addresses

British Waterways Board,
Information Centre,
Melbury House,
Melbury Terrace,
London NW1 6JX
Tel: 01-262 6711

Northwich Area Engineer,
Navigation Road,
Northwich,
Cheshire.
Tel: Northwich (0606) 74321

Canal Societies

If the bug has well and truly bitten you may wish to join the Inland Waterways Association (one of the most powerful non-professional lobbys around) and meet kindred spirits as well as contributing to the waterways movement. Alternatively, you could join one of the individual canal societies which maintain close links with the constituent canals of the FOUR COUNTIES RING: The Shropshire Union Canal Society, Trent & Mersey Canal Society and Staffordshire & Worcestershire Canal Society. Details of the IWA and current membership secretaries of the other canal societies can be obtained from: The Inland Waterways Association, 114 Regent's Park Road, London NW1 8UQ. Tel: 01-586 2556; or the British Waterways Board Information Centre (see above).

If you are a boat owner you could benefit by becoming a member of one of the boat clubs situated on The Ring: Wolverhampton Boat Club, Nantwich & Border Counties Yacht Club, Stoke-on-Trent Boat Club, Stafford Boat Club. Once again further details are available from the British Waterways Board Information Centre.

Licences

Privately owned craft cruising the FOUR COUNTIES RING must have a current British Waterways Board licence whatever the size or nature of the craft. Licences and further details are available from: British Waterways Board, Willow Grange, Church Road, Watford WD1 3QA. Tel: Watford (0923) 26422. Hire boats will already be licenced.

Canal Closures

Canal closures, or stoppages, usually occur between November and early April when maintenance is carried out. Occasionally, however, a stoppage may occur at short notice closing part of the route you intend to cruise. You can check the up to date situation by telephoning Canalphone on 01-723 8486 or checking with your hirebase.

Further Reading

The following books are recommended for those whose appetite for canal knowledge has been whetted, and their authors are acknowledged as source for material found in this publication.

Narrow Boat by L.T.C. Rolt. Eyre Methuen. *The canal masterpiece, a 1939 journey by canal including the whole of The Ring.*

The Inland Waterways of England by L.T.C Rolt. Allen & Unwin. *Well written reference work.*

Thomas Telford by L.T.C. Rolt. Longmans. *Readable bio of the great man with much on Shropshire Union.* (Out of print).

Staffordshire & Worcestershire Canal by J. Ian Langford. Lapal. *Detailed survey of absorbing interest.*

The Trent & Mersey Canal by Peter Lead. Moorland. *Well captioned photo album.*

Journeys of the Sawn by John Liley. Allen & Unwin. *Dead-pan account of journey aboard traditional narrowboat in the Sixties.*